THE POWER OF TAKING THE PLUNGE!

Journey To Your Dream Life by Unlearning What You've Learned

RANDY PERDUE

Empowerment Mentoring Community

www.JohnMaxwellGroup.com/randyperdue

Act as if what you do makes a difference. It does.

~ William James

Published by ImageMeadow

Kindle Edition

ISBN-10 1544621302

ISBN-13 9781544621302

Scripture quotations are from THE NEW KING JAMES VERSION.

I dedicate this book to all who honorably serve our Armed Forces and all who serve and are dedicated to our nation's defence and public safety — May you always be celebrated and protected.

SPECIAL DEDICATION

To Colonel Ted Parks USMC Retired — My whole world changed because of your belief in me, and the books you had me read as a young leader of Marines kindled a flame in my spirit.

To Colonel Bill Truax USMC — Your intersession during the most challenging time of my life literally saved my life. I will forever be indebted. Taking care of your Marines and being a superb leader has never been a challenge for you. It is truly your innate gift.

To all my Marine Corps brothers and sisters who are currently serving or have honorably served our elite team of warriors — Your sacrifices, brotherhood, and relentless determination to succeed against all odds are the ethos that the masses will never understand.

Semper Fidelis!

ACKNOWLEDGEMENTS

There is not enough space in this book to express my heartfelt gratitude to the influencers and marvelous minds whose work has contributed to my own growth over the years and consequently ended up in this book in different forms.

I do want to express a huge thank you to my mentors on the faculty of John Maxwell University. I'm truly humbled to share in the leadership DNA of this dynamic team. It's been over twenty years that I've studied and taught the principles of leadership from John's books and lessons, so it only made sense to me to embrace his vision up close and personal. I'm convinced that the John Maxwell Team will change the world.

I would be remiss if I didn't thank Tom Ziglar and Cindy Ziglar Oates for welcoming me into their family and spending precious time with me. It was over a decade ago that I met their dad and my hero, the legendary Zig Ziglar. His example of character and inspiration will always resonate with me. His handwritten note to me will forever be a treasured keepsake in the Perdue family.

And of course, to Annie and Shirley, my great-grandmother and mother, without their wisdom, strong leadership, and nurturing, none of this would have been possible. They planted in me the seeds of greatness, even though for many years I kept brushing off the fertilizer. I give a lot of credence to Proverbs 22:6. "Train up a child in the way he should go, and when he is old, he will not depart from it." I underlined "old" because it took many failures in my youth and adult life to finally get it. I'm thankful to say that I'm still a work in progress. The stumbling blocks in my life were and continue to be only stepping-stones. "Failure is just an event, not a person." That's one of the greatest lessons they taught me and it's the overarching theme of this book.

Me with the Ziglar Family and my hand on the legendary Zig Ziglar's World-famous, chrome-plated water-pump.

CONTENTS

The Cuz Clan

My first cousins during my birthday 2016. The girl cousins were party poopers.

Left to right:

Brad, Jason, Me, Freddy, Todd. As you can tell, I am the youngest……..HA!

1

INTRODUCTION

The secret of change is to focus all of your energy, not on fighting the old, but on building the new.

~ Socrates

When we look at plant life, we probably don't give much thought to the process of a plant's growth. A seed germinates in the soil and as the plant breaks through the soil and is kissed by the sunlight, photosynthesis occurs and the sun's energy helps nourish the plant. All that the plant requires for survival is light, water, and nutrients from the soil. In the animal kingdom, survival is dependent on instinct. Animals have a built-in survival mechanism. The human species is much more complex and has very different needs. Our brains are very different too. Based on our brain's size in comparison to other species, we have the largest prefrontal cortex. This part of the brain is the gray matter of the anterior part of the frontal lobe. It is highly developed in us and plays a role in the regulation of complex cognitive, emotional, and behavioral functioning. We are without question, God's greatest earthly miracle.

But if a seed stays in its package at the store or lies in a dry place without water and nutrients, it can't fulfill its potential. If an animal is not placed in its right environment or natural habitat, its potential is limited or its extinction is inevitable. The right environment for all creation (man included) is fundamental for growth as well as survival. In the right environment, all creation can fulfill its purpose. Let me emphasize those last few words, "Fulfill its purpose." All creation has a purpose.

I once heard Zig Ziglar give an illustration that I'll never forget. I won't tell it with the same zest as Zig did, but I think you'll get the point. Most of us know that if a house stays vacant for an extended period, it will deteriorate much faster. It's an interesting phenomenon, but it seems that living, breathing human beings who dwell in the house keep it alive. The engineers and flight crews have proven that if a plane stays in the hanger for an extended period, it will wear out faster and the engines won't work properly. But if it flies regularly, it will last longer and require less maintenance. The same thing happens with ships. If a ship stays in the harbor, it will collect barnacles, deteriorate much faster, and become unseaworthy faster than it would sailing the high seas. Here is the main point in this analogy:

(1) Houses are built for living.

(2) Planes are built for flying.

(3) Ships are built for sailing.

(4) And man too was built for a purpose.

All humans are designed for accomplishment. We're engineered for success, and we're endowed with the seeds of greatness. The greatest mistake that man can make is to do nothing at all.

When I heard Zig Ziglar give that analogy, it stuck. I soon came to realize that our greatest danger is our comfort zone. We are either climbing or sliding. There's no in between. We are either getting better or worse. The research is clear that if we do nothing with our three-dimensional being, we begin to deteriorate mentally, physically, and spiritually. We inevitably lessen our days on earth. It's been validated by many studies on longevity that when a person retires from meaningful work or a career, death will occur around the seven-year mark.

Consistently improving in personal development of our three-dimensional beings is the key to long life, joy, happiness, and significance. Most just go with the flow or do what their parents did, or what their reference groups say to do even though they hate it. Christian Evangelist Robert H. Schuller once said, "Even a dead fish can float downstream."

You know in your heart that you're unique. Your DNA proves that uniqueness. In fact, out of the 108 billion plus people who have ever lived, there is no one quite like you. All too often, many never discover their purpose. Many question the meaning of life. They aimlessly wander through life until apathy becomes their comfort zone. American poet and philosopher Henry David Thoreau once said, "Most men live lives of quiet desperation."

In addition to the deadly comfort zone or going with the flow, we are very good at making excuses or blaming others or conditions. It's all about choosing the path of least resistance. The trouble with this mindset is that no one else is going to move you. We all must paddle our own canoe. If you sit back and rest or become a spectator to life, then by default you'll begin to drift along with the flow instead of where you want to go. And water always flows downhill!

John Maxwell says that everything worth having is uphill. And I think that most of us can recognize and accept that when we stop and think about it. When we're comfortable, we don't spend too much time thinking about what we want, where it is, or how we can get it. Instead, we focus on what we don't want and worry about losing what we do have. And guess what? Energy flows where your focus goes.

You literally activate a universal natural law, the Law of Attraction. You eventually get what you think about most of the time. And, yes, that includes the things you don't want. I'm absolutely convinced that you also become what you think about most of the time.

If we all had clear objectives and pursued them continually, I'm sure we would astound ourselves with the capabilities we naturally possess.

Our deepest fear is not that we are inadequate. Our deepest fear is that we are powerful beyond measure. It is our light, not our darkness that most frightens us.

~ Nelson Mandela

Is it possible that Mandela's quote is the reason why more don't make great progress in their lives? I wonder. The statistics are staggeringly disappointing when you look at them. Only 5% of people ever reach financial independence. The majority are unhappy in their job, and nearly everyone argues about money!

Is this all we have to look forward to after a lifetime of experience? What happened to all those hopes and dreams we shared so freely as a child? Where did the hope and wonder of the world go? What happened to the daily happiness that seemed to ooze out of us, infecting everyone around us? Why is true happiness so evasive for so many and what do we have to do to get more of it?

Is it that happiness is a childish fantasy, something that is not meant for grownups! We have plenty of rulebooks and the self-help industry only seems to be helping itself. Those of us who live in the United States need an awakening. The United States makes up less than seven percent of the world population, and yet we consume over ninety percent of the antidepressant drugs that are made worldwide. Why are we increasingly becoming miserable and pessimistic when abundance is all around us? I believe that abundance can be an enemy and can cause us to be complacent. When the cup is full we need to stop pouring. We need to fill another cup, and while filling it, share the filled cup with others.

In John Maxwell's great book, The 15 Invaluable Laws of Growth, he tells a story that I just love. As the fortuneteller reads the man's fortune she says, "You'll be poor and miserable until you are 40 years old." "Then what happens?" asks the man with a glint of hope. "Then you get used to it!"

I love the prophetic brilliance in that story — not for everyone of course, but for many people. It is sad but oh so true, isn't it? Thucydides said, "The secret to happiness is freedom. And the secret to freedom is courage." Surely this applies to individuals just as much as it applies to nations, races or communities. How many people do you know who have the courage to pursue flexibility and freedom in their lives in an appropriate way, and do you think they are happy?

In the Bible, there is a verse that says, "Narrow is the gate and difficult is the way which leads to life, and there are few who find it." Could that mean peace and happiness are indeed a scarce thing?

I believe happiness is an inside job. It's not something you get from external circumstances or things. It is the result of what's going on inside. A mentor of mine said that there is almost a 100% correlation between happiness and awareness or levels of consciousness. The more 'aware person' can be happy almost completely detached from externals while the unaware person is unhappy almost no matter what. Nothing you can do for them will make them happy.

I'm convinced that the late Earl Nightingale was one of the wisest men in the 20th Century. He said that happiness is the progressive realization of a worthy ideal. Progressive is the optimum word I want to emphasize. If you achieve a goal, it's only the beginning of your happiness. It is the constant and never-ending improvement in all the dimensions of our lives that I believe brings inner joy, peace, and happiness.

Do you have a philosophy on life and happiness? How committed are you to this belief? Is it realistic? Is it logical? And most importantly of all, is it helping you? Whatever your philosophy is on happiness, taking responsibility for your growth, having the courage to face life and get the best out of whatever experiences you face is undoubtedly the best strategy for growth for every aspect of your nature.

I hope in some small way this book can help you in that pursuit by giving you a formula for extracting more of the rich marrow out of life. This process works for everyone who applies it.

Life is a wonderful adventure. You are already very good at it, but you can get better. Every effort you make to develop and grow through your life experiences will inevitably be reflected in your experience of the world.

It certainly is true that we all get experience, but not all of us stop and think about what we can learn from these experiences. All too often we carry on banging our head against the same wall without realizing it is of our own making, and not only do we not have to bang our head against it, but it's not actually there at all.

Wherever you are on your journey, whatever the circumstances of your life, and however you feel about it all at the moment of reading these words, I want to reach out to you and let you know that you are a wonderful human being capable of far more than you ever thought possible. You have more potential than you can ever dream of using. You are perfectly imperfect, just like everyone else. You are no better than anyone else and no worse. You are doing great, but you can do better, and you should!

.......You are God's greatest earthly miracle!

You are the only one who can use your ability. It is an awesome responsibility.

~ Zig Ziglar

ACTION EXERCISES

What would a dream life look like for you?

What would you do if you knew you couldn't fail?

If you were to leave this world right now, would you be content with what you've done here, and with what you've become?

When it's all over and someone is summing up your life and the kind of person you are, what do you think they would say?

What would you like for them to say?

Write out the answers or think about them, or better yet, discuss them with a loved one.

2

WHERE ARE YOU STUCK?

There are two primary choices in life: to accept conditions as they exist, or accept the responsibility for changing them.

~ Denis Waitley

At a very young age, I thought that being tough was the most important thing for a boy to prove his manhood. TV and movie heroes like the Six Million Dollar Man, played by Lee Majors and John Wayne, the Marines' Marine were just some of the examples that fueled many boy's motivation.

My mom also appeased me by buying a weight set for me at the age of ten. I began putting most of my focus on getting stronger and tougher. The one thing that I totally ignored was other sports.

I once considered myself to be an excellent basketball player. Compared to the other boys in my small community, I felt confident in my skills as a basketball player. The legendary Jerry West was most boys' hero. He too was a West Virginian who left the small town of Cabin Creek to become a famous NBA basketball star.

By the age of twelve, I realized that basketball was not going to be my ambitious pursuit. I quickly lost interest. I had put my interests in other things (some not good) and my friends kept getting better at the sport. As a kid with no dad to influence me, I just took it upon myself to stick with what I was good at doing — fighting and getting tougher. Even though I managed to get my butt kicked, I was convinced that being tough was my calling.

I want to point out something before I tell the rest of this story. Statistically, a boy that grows up without a father has a lot of disadvantages, and unfortunately, many become "'juvenile delinquents." That label is offensive to me. Even though I was well on my way to fulfilling that role, I had many Godly men in my family and in my community who set the right example. Labeling a kid has deep emotional and psychological ramifications. We should always tell our youth that they have boundless and genius potential.

My self-esteem was greatly suffering because I was failing in so many other areas. I am so thankful that the drug Ritalin was not on the market because the school faculty would have had me on it within the first week of the 1st grade. I'll discuss the insanity of our public-school system in a later chapter. By the age of fourteen, the only other thing that really had my full interest was....well, you may have guessed it, "girls." My problem was that my reputation prevented a lot of dads from allowing their precious daughters to associate with me. And then it happened, I met Debbie, a girl who moved to West Virginia from Ohio.

Fortunately, her dad, who was nicknamed, "Ham," saw me for what I was; a boy who needed a man's example. In the very short time I spent with him and his wife Patsy and other two daughters, Brenda and Kim, I learned more about being a man than I realized. I was a grown man myself before I realized the influence he had on me. The main lesson that he taught me was that anything worth doing takes patience and perseverance. That repetition is the mother of skill. He never used those exact words, but his example was clear. He was truly the example of a real man. But like all teens, the puppy love vanished, and Debbie kicked me to the curb. I was so devastated, not because of losing her, but because of losing the family that I had grown to love and admire. I've since become dear friends with Debbie, (and yes Debbie, you know I've forgiven you, even though you totally destroyed my life — Only kidding!)

It was such a joy to visit Ham after I became an adult. Just a few years ago, Ham left this life on earth, and I'm glad I had the opportunity to attend his funeral. His son-in-law, Don Tompkins and I, (both former Marines) folded the American Flag that was draped over his coffin, and I had the distinct honor to present it to his wife, Pasty. As I write these words, Patsy (who always called me her son) went to be with Ham in Glory less than two weeks ago. My only regret is that I had the opportunity to spend more time with them, but I always had lame excuses that I was too busy.

As Ham taught me, constant improvement and focus are the keys. That can be difficult when we have so many distractions, especially a hyperactive guy like me. I remember going hunting with him once, and he gave me a lesson on trees. He pointed at and named every tree in the forest. That literally blew my mind. And, oh what a hunter and fisherman he was. He once killed three wild turkeys with a single shot by putting some type of feed in a straight line on the ground, and while the turkeys were eating it, he made a clicking sound, and the turkeys raised their heads in unison, and "Bang!" one shot, three kills. Many hunters who read this may be saying, "So what," but I was fascinated, to say the least.

I never adopted the patience for hunting, and I still struggle with being patient at times on other tasks. However, I have developed the awareness that success in most things takes patience, and success is not a matter of luck nor is it an accident. Dr. Denis Waitley once said that luck is an acronym, L.U.C.K. laboring under correct knowledge. The granddaddy law, Cause and Effect, totally debunks the accident or luck theory. If we want to get good at anything, it takes an internal commitment to stick with it. Like Randy Perdue missing his great opportunity to be an NBA star. Why? because he didn't stick with it. I laugh as I say that because it brings up another key point. None of us can be masters at everything.

As I mentioned in the Introduction, there have been over 108 billion people to walk on this earth and there will never be another you. We all have what I believe is a divine purpose. Each of us has the potential to be excellent in at least one or two areas. We can absolutely be in the top ten percent of any career field if we have the ingredients of patience, discipline, and persistence. But more importantly, we can be in the top one or two percent if we add the ingredient of natural talent. We all have natural talents, but most never recognize them, or even if we do, we never develop them to the fullest potential.

Like losing my basketball skill, personal growth takes patience, discipline, and persistence. "What you don't use, you lose." We know this intellectually. Like Zig Ziglar's analogy of the house, plane, and ship, we must always be in a perpetual state of growth. If we have the knowledge and the recipe for success, what do you think are our greatest roadblocks? I believe I have the answers. In fact, I get excited when I think about the answers because they are so simple. Even the latest neuroscience experts have discovered these simple yet profound roadblocks that keep most people living mediocre lives. The simple truth that neuroscience has proven is that our brains are lazy.

I had the opportunity last year to go to the Neuro-Leadership Summit in New York City. Dr. David Rock is the founder of the Neuro-Leadership Institute. There I was, Randy Perdue, the hillbilly from West Virginia among some of the greatest minds and corporate executives in the world. I felt like a weenie in a steakhouse. I bought Dr. Rock's book (got it autographed of course) called, Your Brain at Work. I also had an inspiring and very informative conversation with Dr. Josh Davis, author of the book, Two Awesome Hours – Science-Based Strategies to Harness Your Best Time and Get Your Most Important Work Done. During his presentation, he explained the functions of each part of the brain, but what interested me the most was the fact that he said that our brains were lazy. The neuro-networks with the help of what are called synapse, which are like conductors that pass electrical and chemical signals between the neurons, choose a path and attempt to stay on that path. In other words, they choose the path of least resistance. That explained volumes to me about human nature.

Have you ever witnessed a woman who has been in an abusive relationship, and she either continues in the abuse or leaves the man only to find another abusive man? Most would question her sanity, right? The problem is that there may be several factors as the root cause, but perhaps the two most common are (1) The fear of the unknown. Simply put, the comfort zone. She knows and is familiar with that person. You may have heard the expression, 'The devil you know is better than the devil you don't.' (2) The phenomenon called the Law of Attraction. I know that this is a hard pill to swallow for some, and I don't mean to offend, but the fact is that she attracts that type of person. Perhaps she repeatedly holds onto the thoughts of not being worthy of someone better. Whatever thoughts permeate her conscious and unconscious mind will bring forth the fruit of those thoughts. I only wanted to give you this as an example.

When we look at the comfort zone due to how our brain operates, it's pretty clear as to why some choose to live miserable lives. Whether it's running from job to job, not working at all, or working in environments that they absolutely despise, the brain has been programmed to resist change. I'm convinced that only babies with wet diapers like change. But, there is good news. We all have the power to move in another direction. We are in a constant state of change whether we're aware of it or not. We're either getting better, or we're getting worse. The choice is ours.

The problem with the world is the intelligent people are full of doubts and the stupid people are full of confidence.

~ Charles Bukowski

Here's to the crazy ones, the misfits, the rebels, the troublemakers, the round pegs in the square holes... the ones who see things differently -- they're not fond of rules... You can quote them, disagree with them, glorify or vilify them, but the only thing you can't do is ignore them because they change things... they push the human race forward, and while some may see them as the crazy ones, we see genius, because the ones who are crazy enough to think that they can change the world, are the ones who do.

~ Steve Jobs

Me with Sis at the beginning of my marksmanship training.

As a young Marine 1977

ACTION EXERCISES

Where are you stuck in your life?

Which particular fears are holding you back?

Are there things you want that you are not going after?

When was the last time you did something you've never done before?

Write out the answers, or think about them, or better yet, discuss them with a loved one.

3

WHO IS GOING TO DO IT FOR YOU?

Responsibility is the price of freedom.

~ Elbert Hubbard

I'd like to begin this chapter by asking you, "Who do you think the greatest American philosopher in the 1970's was?" I'm convinced that it was the boxing legend, Rocky Balboa. Now, before you judge my sanity, hear me out. For those of you who recall the Rocky movie series with Sylvester Stallone as Rocky, you'll get my point.

In the first movie, Rocky was considered a nobody that ended up fighting the World Heavyweight Champion Apollo Creed. In one of the scenes, a fifteen-year-old girl in the Philadelphia neighborhood was walking down the street with Rocky. He'd just observed her hanging out with some thugs. He managed to get her attention and consequently got her away from the crowd of unruly youths. He started giving her a lecture that illustrates a significant point for you to consider. He began by saying, "If you hang out with smart people, you're going to be smart; if you hang out with stupid people, you're going to be stupid." He then gave her more contrasting comparisons throughout their short encounter. The girl passively agrees with Rocky until she arrives at her apartment. Once she entered the front screen door, closed it, then turned facing Rocky, she uttered, "Up yours, Rocky!" She then made the universal gesture by swinging her arm and bending the elbow swiftly as her middle finger extended. I think you get the picture. But the point of this profound wisdom that Rocky shared with the girl is what I need to share. "You do become part of what you are around."

I once heard Brian Tracy say that we become the average of the five people we spend the most time with. I'm convinced he's right. Rocky Balboa had the secret of success. Our environment of our social reference group has a tremendous impact on our failures and our successes. Brian went on to say that if you're the smartest person in your group, you need to find another group. Your growth and success will be stifled.

What I find interesting is that when we start to move our minds in another direction, when we become aware that our thoughts are evolving and our ideals begin to change, our current reference group tends to get uncomfortable. Remember, only babies with wet diapers like change. Even if your social network of friends and loved-ones appear to be happy for you when you begin to progress they will consciously and unconsciously attempt to sabotage your success. They don't purposely want to hurt your feelings, they are simply trying to stay in their comfort zone.

I'm quite certain that once you look back on your past, you soon recognize that you've changed your social networks. I can't even imagine engaging in past networks of what I considered to be my buddies. I'm not saying that I'm superior to those in my past, it's just that my interests have evolved differently. I first recognized that after I'd been on active duty in the U.S. Marine Corps.

Every young man and woman who join the Corps, go through a noticeable transformation, both physically, mentally, and spiritually. As the Marine Corps recruiting billboards proudly proclaim, "The Change is Forever!" I believe that to be true. However, I have witnessed a few 'former' Marines who've been inundated in cultural norms for so long that a lot of the Marine Corps image is unrecognizable. This analogy is an example of how social networks play a significant role in our success or failure.

After I joined the Marine Corps, it didn't take very long to recognize that I had very little in common with my former social networks. It was abundantly clear to me that my friends back home felt a bit uneasy around me. When I would attempt any repartee or normal conversation, I'd get that stare which clearly meant to me, 'you've changed, and you make me feel uncomfortable.' After spending twenty years on active duty, it became extremely obvious that I had changed considerably.

Friday, August 8, 1997, I was standing on a parade field as a Marine Corps marching band and a battalion of Marines were marching in front of me to bid me farewell for my retirement ceremony — the ceremonial 'Pass in Review.' The drum major spun his staff, then rendered a hand salute. I distinctly recall his white glove and precise, slow rendering of his salute. As tears streamed down my face while returning the salute, I quickly became aware that I was leaving what I believed to be the most elite military organization on the planet. Most importantly, I knew that in those columns of men and women marching before me, none would ever hesitate to put their lives on the line to protect me, and they knew I'd do the same for them. Eight days later, my world drastically changed. I walked in the front door of West Virginia's Maximum Security Prison. Let me clarify; not as a prisoner, but as an employee.

Shortly before retirement from the Marine Corps, I went home on vacation and spoke to retired Army Lieutenant Colonel Chuck Kinder, who used to play football for West Virginia University. He was the kicker on the team back in the 60's and the only kicker in WVU history, or perhaps in any college team's history to wear the number 100. It just so happened that he was on the team during West Virginia's Centennial celebration of becoming one of the 50 states. Anyway, Chuck worked for the state's Division of Personnel at the time, and I'll never forget the advice that he gave me. He enthusiastically said, "Randy, just get your foot in the door anywhere in state government, and with your background and leadership experience, you'll write your own ticket." He went on to say that the state is always hungry for leaders.

On the 16th of August, I began my training at the prison. I didn't have the red ruby slippers to click like Dorothy did on The Wizard of Oz. I did realize that I wasn't in Kansas anymore. I guess I can relate my feelings to how Rip Van Winkle must have felt when he woke from his long-extended sleep. It was truly a cultural shock. I didn't have any idea how much a negative environment would physically affect me. Most experts agree that drastic changes in anyone's environment have negative biochemical consequences.

I used to brag about the fact that I never got sick; no colds, no headaches, no illnesses whatsoever for over seven years. I tell this story to audiences to illustrate how an environment can have a profound effect on you mentally, physically, and spiritually. From late 1989 to the fall of 1997, the only thing that affected me was a back injury. In 1989, while stationed in Okinawa, Japan, I slipped the lowest disc in my back because I was showing off in front of two

Japanese girls who ran their car into a ditch. This tough Marine suddenly was turned into a helpless cripple as I lifted the tiny car from its entrapment. Other than the back injury, no other sickness or disease entered my body until I began my career in the prison system. Within six months of employment, I had a headache at least once per week, and I had the flu twice. I knew that it had everything to do with my new environment. When I ask the question to audiences as to why the sudden change in my health, they don't hesitate to say, 'stress.' I then go on to say, "Do you not think that a Marine deals with stressful situations?" They seem to be stumped when I ask that question, but they obviously know the correct answer. Our common sense tells us that life-threatening situations are stressful to anyone. So, what made the big difference in my immune system?

There is nothing better than getting shot at and missed. It's really great.

~ U.S. Secretary of Defense James Mattis-Marine Corps General (Retired)

A close friend of mine, Dr. Tracy Reveal, introduced me to Author Simon Sinek's books. One was entitled, Start with Why and the other, Leaders Eat Last. I found both of his books to be beyond fascinating. However, Leaders Eat Last really resonated with me. He put an extensive amount of research into it, and it scientifically proves what I believed was only my theory before reading his book. Stress does weaken you and can literally stop the immune system. Simon describes what the hormone cortisol does. It is the stress hormone that is released in the brain when danger or a threat exists. Getting shot at is a very stressful situation, but it happens, and then it's typically over in a short time. The main function of the cortisol being released is to alarm us that danger is present. When the danger leaves, so too the cortisol leaves your system.

Remember when I was describing the formation of Marines marching? I said that I knew they would put their lives on the line to protect me. That's the evidence Simon is referring to. When you have trust in the people around you, cortisol won't do its job. However, if you're in an environment where you can't trust the person to your left or to your right, it's like you're walking around with a cortisol drip, very much like a patient who has a morphine drip constantly entering the bloodstream. The sad part of my new environment was that it wasn't only the inmates that you couldn't trust, it was the staff as well. I was not enjoying the changes that I was experiencing in me. I became passionate to change the prison-work environment and it's still a tedious and tasking process. Changing any culture is tremendously challenging.

The lack of trust does affect increases in cortisol production, and a lack of trust is nothing more than subtle fear (continuous fear in small doses). Chapter Five will be helpful for you in giving you a deeper understanding of that 'four letter word.'

As we discussed in the last chapter, no one really likes change, particularly change that happens to you, as opposed to change that you choose and drive yourself.

There's a certain dynamic to any club or group when everyone maintains the cohesiveness of thought, actions, and opinions. If a change occurs in one member, it threatens the status quo for everyone. This is especially true of a 'negative' type group. Many organizations have what I like to refer to as the duck pond. There is a group that is always quacking, moaning, and complaining, but they're never willing to step out and take responsibility. The old saying, 'Birds of a feather flock together' is so profoundly true, and Rocky Balboa was indeed a prophet.

If your life is not where you know it should be. That's really a good place to be. Every change for the better begins with thought. But here's the warning that goes with it. People you love as well as those you are indifferent about will try and keep you stuck where you are, consciously or often unconsciously because they don't understand or they don't want change to happen to them.

Put another way, it means that when you decide that you want something, you need to overcome the gravitational pull of everyone in your environment because they don't want you to have it! I know that sounds crazy, but it is true. It's not that you can't get them on board, often you can, but you need to grow and take them with you, not expect them to help you get there. Some of them will accept the new you, but many will not.

Everyone in your life has some kind of vested unconscious desire for you to carry on as you are, so if you want to change, no one is going to do it for you. We all must take complete and utter responsibility for ourselves. Expecting others to do it for us, or even to be on board with us, just sets us up for disappointment.

One day I was fishing on a dock off the coast of South Carolina when I came upon an elderly man who was trapping crabs. I watched as he pulled the crab cage out of the water, and it appeared that several crabs were trapped inside. What I found interesting was the fact that there was no lid on the trap. In ignorance, I asked the gentleman how the crabs manage to stay in the cage with no lid. He chuckled as my embarrassment began to be exposed, and he said, "You don't need one. Once you have one in the cage, any others that enter it are pulled down by the others that are trapped." I never gave it much thought at the time, but it did seem strange to me. Now when I think about it, I realize what a great analogy to use when it comes to change. Anytime you try to step out of the norm, others will extend their pinchers, latch on, and attempt to pull you back down. They may very well love you, but they want you to stay in the trap with them. Misery does love company.

Taking responsibility is the first step of many different systems of help and change. For as long as you believe that someone or something else is responsible for your growth, nothing is going to change. The world will continue to hold up the same merciless mirror, reflecting back the same life experience until you agree to take the helm and chart your own course.

If you are not living the life you dream of, and most people aren't, it's not the fault of your parent's, your spouse, or your children. It's not the fault of the government, the economy, the weatherman, or anything or anyone else's.

We have all been gifted with the ability to choose what to do in any and every moment. Different choices take us in different directions. But with that marvelous gift of free will comes the responsibility for the decisions we make. In many ways, it's as simple as that!

"Insanity is doing the same things over and over again expecting different results."

~ Albert Einstein

You take your life in your own hands and what happens? A terrible thing, no one to blame!

~ Erica Jong

ACTION EXERCISES

Who do you depend on in your life?

Why do you depend on them?

Are there important things in your life that you are waiting for other people to deliver? Why?

What would it take for you to do what you are waiting for them to do?

Write the answers, or think about them, or better yet, discuss them with a loved one.

4

WHAT IS IT YOU WANT, I MEAN REALLY?

Goals that are casually set are freely abandoned at the first obstacle.

~ Zig Ziglar

How many times have you started something that you felt at the time was a pretty worthy goal, but after the first sign of failure, you just threw in the towel? I know I've done that numerous times in my life. Or, perhaps you were motivated to try something because a close friend or relative encouraged you. You have, and so have I. Sometimes it works out, and sometimes it doesn't. Sometimes we need that person to kick us in the butt to get us moving. We all have been inspired to try to capture the zeal of what others experience. There is absolutely nothing wrong with having those experiences. Often, they lead us to where we really want to go.

I remember when I trained for my first 26.2-mile marathon. I set the goal, and within six months I was ready to experience the worst pain that I think I have ever experienced. For those distance runners out there, you know the term, "The Wall." I still managed to finish in under four hours. My goal was to just survive. I hit what is called 'the runner's wall' at the twenty-two-mile mark. What I found shocking was the fact that at nineteen miles, I had a surge of energy (endorphin rush) that propelled me to start running under a seven-minute pace. The endorphins quickly left my bloodstream as well as most of the nutrients required to put one foot in front of the other. After about a week of recovery, I was back at it. My brain's release of endorphins (God's natural pain medication) and the reward chemical dopamine was too pleasurable to just stop. I'm not suggesting that you run a marathon, but accomplishing that type of goal is very powerful.

Success breeds success. Each time we accomplish something that takes hard work and discipline, a neuro-pathway or track is set in the brain like a template. Thus, we are driven to continue on the pathway of success because of the incredible feeling it gives us. The interesting thing though is that running that marathon was my goal. It was personal to me. You won't be successful if you're trying to reach someone else's goal.

I remember when I was training, my daughter, Randi, would want to run along beside me. When she was about six years old, she'd put her little shoes on and run beside me in the military housing area where we lived. She would take at least three paces to my one, but she'd run over a mile before getting tuckered out. The training was rewarding for her because after she started school, she could run faster than every boy in her class. She was pretty cocky about it too until she reached third grade. At one of her recesses, she raced a bunch of boys on the school's track and a boy beat her. She got so disappointed that she ended up quitting her running career (so to speak). Her mother and I would try to encourage her to no avail. I believe that was the first time she experienced defeat, and she'll admit today at age 35, that she was a very sore loser.

Do you think that if her mother and I forced her to continue it would have done any good? I think you know the answer to that. The goal had to be hers and hers alone. She had to own it. I have witnessed parents forcing their children into things only to discover their resentment. I tried that with my son Chris on several worthy objectives, and even after he became an adult, he would remind me of my Marine Corps Drill Instructor tactics. The funny thing is that I don't remember a lot of the details, and I've tried to convince him that he as just adding the extra drama to make the story sound worse than it really was.

There's an old saying, "No one washes a rental car!" It's true, isn't it? If you don't own it, you just don't feel the same way about it. Don't let anyone else dictate your goals for you. You must find things that you want to pursue! You are worth it. You deserve it, and as you progressively grow to the point where you achieve your goals and dreams, you will attain more of that seemingly elusive thing called happiness.

Remember what I said earlier in the Introduction Chapter about Earl Nightingale's quote, "Happiness is the progressive realization of a worthy ideal." It is a funny thing that most people never really think about. What it is they want? I mean really want. They will list off the things that they don't want very quickly, and because of their mental focus and dominant thoughts, what they don't want is what they get.

Lora Goodrich has a training program called, Seeing Red Cars. In the video, it gives participants great illustrations of getting what they don't want because that is where a lot of people's focus is. She points out in the video that when you buy a red car or anything for that matter, you start seeing it everywhere. We've all experienced that haven't we? Ladies go out and buy a new outfit, men buy a new toy, and then they experience seeing others with the same thing. What is also profound is that you get what you don't want too. Energy flows to where your thoughts go, and like waving a magic wand, "Poof, there it is!"

Therefore, when you set a goal, it must be positive, as well as personal. I like referring to Brian Tracy's class on goal setting. He says that the three "P's" are the fastest and most effective way to set goals. Personal, Positive, and Present tense is the key. Your brain accepts the information you feed it. Even the words we use have power. You should never set a goal with negative words like quit, stop, debt, etc. Let me give you an example:

Instead of saying, "I will quit smoking."

Replace that statement with, "I am a non-smoker."

The key is the present tense. The subconscious has difficulty with a future focus. It responds more quickly to the 'now.' You may be thinking, "Isn't that lying?" I used to tell audiences, "Lie with integrity." Then I heard Brain Tracy say that you're not really telling a lie, you're just telling the truth in advance. What a brilliant way to put it. So, instead of saying, "I will lose fifty pounds"…..say, I weigh 150 pounds." That's of course if your current weight is 200 pounds. You are training the subconscious to make your words a reality.

I believe the subconscious mind, or as some call it the unconscious mind, is very much like a computer program. I've heard that comparison by numerous experts. Your subconscious responds to your instructions. If you write down a goal or speak it aloud, it goes to work on bringing the goal into your reality. That's why I tell audiences, "Never say anything about yourself that you don't want to be true." I then give them instructions on reprogramming their internal computer, so that it's cleared of all the viruses that they or others have put into it. I close the session by quoting a poem that was written by Denis Waitley. He called it his RU-ME-2, not to be confused with R2D2 on Star Wars. Forgive me if I don't quote the exact wording of Dr. Waitley's work, but I think you'll appreciate it.

(Reprogramming the Subconscious)

I have a little robot that goes around with me.

I tell it what I'm thinking; I tell it what I see.

I tell my little robot all its hopes and fears.

It listens and remembers everything it hears.

At first, my little robot would follow my command.

But after years of training, he's gotten out of hand.

He doesn't care what's right or wrong or what is false or true.

No matter what I try now, he tells me what to do.

Also, using the word "I" is crucial. It is the only word in the dictionary specific to you. It makes it personal. It's also important to give your goals a completion date. By giving them a deadline, you ignite the subconscious and activate the new neuro networks.

Many experts in the field of psychology say that it takes about twenty-one days to create a new habit. It's different for everyone, but if you commit to doing a new empowering discipline, commit to it for thirty days. The experts also say that you can't really break a bad habit unless you replace it with a good one. The brain will detect the void and try to replace the void with something else or go back to the old habit (the comfort zone). You are the one to control that. In fact, the only things that we truly have any control over are the thoughts we think on a regular basis.

The President of the John Maxwell Group, Paul Martinelli, often says, "Most people say they want a lot more than they actually do, and they settle for far less than they could easily get."

What are some of the things you truly want? Give yourself permission to stop and think about this question. Don't include the things you need. There is far less motivational drive involved with needs. I want you to think of the things that ignite your passion — the things that give you that surge of energy and a feeling of purpose. These are your worthy goals and dreams, and I've got good news for you concerning them. You don't have to settle for a life that excludes them. You just have to pinpoint what they actually are. They must be specific. Having a lot of money is not a goal. You have to write down the specific amount. If losing weight is your goal, write down the specific number.

I love this goal-setting acronym: S.M.A.R.T. I have seen different words for each of the letters for the purpose of setting goals, but my favorite are these:

Specific

Measurable

Actionable

Realistic

Timebound

Specific. I think one of the main benefits of being really clear on the goal is that the desire to achieve or attain something specific really pulls us forward. It lures us into growth. Going after something we don't actually know how to achieve (because we haven't paved the way yet) forces us to tackle new situations and challenges in order to continue the process of growth in our lives. It forces us to take advantage of opportunities that we, perhaps, didn't even see before, or discounted as being too risky.

Going after something specific we want forces us to pick ourselves up after things go wrong and to try something else. Indifference does none of these things. Ambiguity doesn't either. That's why it's important to write down your goal. Experts in the field of neuro (brain) research are discovering that there is a direct correlation between your hand and the brain. If you write out a goal or take notes in class rather than type or text. I suppose the brain absorbs or digests it better (my layman's terms).

Measurable. First, look at where you are or your current condition. Then, after you have the specific goal in mind, measure your daily or weekly progress. Remember to write it out clearly. Something magical seems to happen in the brain when we see it clearly. If you can't write it in your own words, then you missed out on clarity. So, make the goal specific and measure the progress (write it down).

Actionable. You must take some immediate action once you have set the goal. It should be incremental action. Remember this, "By the yard it's hard, by the inch it's a cinch."

Realistic. The goal should be just out of reach but not completely out of sight. It must be believable to you. This is where your faith plays a major role.

Timebound. Give your goal a realistic deadline. If you set a goal to weigh 150 pounds and you currently weigh 200 pounds, getting it done in a week is not realistic, is it? Perhaps liposuction would do it, but that is probably not wise.

The things that we want can be large or small. They can take a few hours to achieve or a lifetime. The bigger the goal and the longer it takes to achieve, the more order it introduces into our lives. The most successful people on the planet have a long-term perspective.

Order is heaven's first law.

For us to achieve anything meaningful, we need order and movement. One without the other doesn't really work, does it?

In James Allen's great book, As a Man Thinketh, there is a chapter about thought and purpose. At the beginning of this chapter, he reminds us, "Until thought is linked with purpose, there is no intelligent accomplishment."

So, the order that comes from a clear objective permeates every aspect of our life. Order to our thinking. Order to our actions. And order to our results.

When I talk to people about this, most of them can quickly see that order comes from a clear direction, objective, or compass bearing. What they truly struggle with though is the answer to life's greatest question, 'What is my purpose?'

Peter Drucker said something marvelous, "Only musicians, mathematicians and a few early maturing people, their numbers limited, know what they want to do from an early age. The rest of us have to find out."

As you embark upon this journey of 'finding out' your life purpose, you're going to have to push past a lot of things that hold most people back from this journey.

Fear will try to creep in and tell you, 'oh, those are just pipe-dreams. You need to be grateful for what you have. Not everyone is marked for greatness. Just stay where you are. Do what has the least amount of risk.' Essentially, all of these fear-based thoughts are attempting to convince you to settle for a life that is far less than you are capable of being. Is that what you want? Of course not.

Then you're going to have to learn to face your fears. They will always be there. They'll be waiting for your weakest moments so they can swoop in and tell you to give up. But when you're willing to pull the mask off fear, you'll see that all the things you are tempted to worry about are ridiculous.

Yes, you might fall down. You might look foolish. You might make a huge mistake. But the other side of that looks like this:

You'll get back up.

You'll learn from mistakes.

You'll become an inspiration to others.

To me, that's worth the trials, the mistakes, the obstacles and even the temporary foolish moments.

Peter Drucker also said, "People who don't take risks generally make about two big mistakes a year. People who do take risks make about two big mistakes a year."

I'd rather make my mistakes actively engaging in the pursuit of my goals and dreams. How about you?

My son Chris and daughter Randi

ACTION EXERCISES

Have you ever written out your goals?

Make a commitment to find a quiet place in the morning and ask yourself, "What do I really want in life?"

Pray. Ask God, "What is my purpose, and what should I do with my life that would be a service to others, bring glory to you, and benefit me?" Then in silence, listen to that still voice within.

List some specific things to do to get the momentum going.

Begin to make a list of what you want:

1. in your relationships.
2. in your health.
3. in your finances.
4. in your career.
5. in your spiritual walk.
6. in your learning.
7. in your hobbies or personal joy.

5

WHAT IS REAL, THE DANGER OR THE FEAR?

We cannot live better than in seeking to be become better.
~ Socrates

I find that the research into the studies of fear is fascinating. Babies only have two responses to fear; a fear response to loud noises and a fear response to the threat of falling. So, what does that leave for us to conclude? It must mean that all other fear is a learned behavior.

It's been very interesting and thought-provoking to me throughout my own research in human behavior, psychology, neuroscience, and leadership that we all develop differently. I remember that there was a time in my young adult years that I honestly believed that I had all the answers to effective leadership, motivation, and success. All that my friends, family, and coworkers had to do is apply my strategies, and their lives would drastically change for the better.

I couldn't understand why everyone wasn't interested in the same things that I was. I also had a challenge with understanding why many had so many phobias. I have discovered though that there are healthy types of fear. An example of that would be being trapped in a car on the railroad tracks and a train is just seconds away from crashing into you. I know that using that type of example is extreme, but I find it interesting that some things that people fear don't even hit my radar, so to speak.

One fear that I find fascinating is the fear of public speaking. It's the number one fear according to some research. Some would rather run through a burning building than to stand in front of an audience to deliver a simple message.

I remember when my daughter, Randi, had to say, "To be honest" in an auditorium filled with parents. She was a Brownie at the time (a younger version of the Girl Scouts). I feel bad that I didn't prepare her for the experience. Her mother and I were anxiously awaiting her stage appearance, with dad holding the camcorder. The little girl that came before her annunciated her line with confidence. She said, "To be Cheerful." Then came Randi. With a fear on her face that I had never witnessed, she attempted to utter out her line. She did well with the first two words, "To be," but she totally forgot the word "Honest." She attempted to say the word, "Cheerful," which was the little girl's line before her. She couldn't even get the word out correctly. I was standing there with the camcorder in hand and you could visibly watch the visual playback bouncing up and down because of my laughing.

Randi didn't find anything humorous about that event. She literally froze on stage. To this day, she has no desire to ever do public speaking. Although anyone can learn to get over that fear, she like many has chosen to hang onto it. What was really funny to me was the fact that at her speaking debut that evening, her two front baby teeth were missing. It would have been much easier to say the word "Honest" than it would "Cheerful." The bottom line is that she learned that fear, and daddy didn't help matters.

The developmental stages and the fears a child learns as he or she develops are very interesting.

At around eight to ten months, babies begin to understand 'object permanence.' Before this point, if something is in their awareness it exists. When it is removed from their awareness it ceases to exist. But after this stage, the idea that something is still in existence but just not there at that moment occurs. This leads to other trains of thought, like, 'Where has daddy gone?

When will he be back?' This is connected to separation anxiety.

I remember traveling from San Antonio, Texas to Quantico, Virginia to attend six weeks of leadership training. I had never been away from my youngest, Randi, for more than ten to twelve hours since her birth. She was about two years of age at the time. When I returned to San Antonio, she and her mother, Cathy, were awaiting my arrival at the airport. When Cathy pointed me out to her and said, "There's daddy!", the look on my little girl's face was a look that I'll never forget. There were a few seconds that I was unrecognizable to her. As her mom was holding her, I reached for her, and once she was in my embrace, she began to rub my face with her little hand as she stared into my eyes. She latched on to me as though she would never let go. Our relationship was forever changed after that trip.

One of the other key developmental stages for children occurs with the development of the imagination. Every parent notices a difference in the play of their child if they pay attention.

They start making stuff up. They start lying! What is interesting about this stage is that fears can then come from sources that can't be seen. Things like the bogeyman and things that go bump in the night!

My oldest child, Chris, has forgiven me, (I think.) I've looked back on the past at some of the practical jokes I would play on him, and it troubles me some. Although it was funny at the time, I'm sure to him, I was inflicting cruel and unusual punishment.

I remember being with him on a dock at night fishing on the coastline of Beaufort, South Carolina. The moon was full — not a cloud in the sky. Suddenly, a school of small fish swam under the dock. The pattern in the water was at least ten meters wide. You could easily see the movement of the swimming fish in unison. I looked down, pointed, and yelled out, "Water monster!" I then took off in a run as if the monster was coming after us. He screamed in fear and followed me as fast as his little legs could move. Alarmed by Chris' frightened reaction, I immediately told him that I was only joking and that it was just a school of small fish. He must have been twelve years old at the time, and to this day he has no reservations in telling that story to his friends in my presence merely for the purpose of embarrassing me for my child abuse tactics. At age 38, I'm not sure if he thinks about water monsters when he's on the ocean, but I'm certain that he will never forget that fear I instilled in him. Today Chris is extremely creative, and I'm sure he has thought that if we could have made a Reality TV series titled, "Bad Dads," I would have won an Emmy.

It is a normal part of children's development to go through these different stages of fear. They don't need dads to force them through it. However, what is important is that they are transitory. As children learn to overcome these fears, they learn that they can deal with life. They can overcome challenges and say to themselves, "That wasn't so bad after all!"

As adults, though, if we are stuck with a certain irrational fear, it may or may not be a problem. If it is stopping us from getting what we want, then maybe it is a problem to be worked on and overcome.

It’s an interesting thing about fear; we put total faith in it. We feel that something is going to happen, and we then trust that thought implicitly. We allow it to control our thinking, our feelings, and our actions…and therefore our results.

Perhaps this is what Franklin Roosevelt was talking about in his inaugural address when he said, “The only thing we have to fear is fear itself.”

If you think about it, it’s interesting because the fear we experience doesn’t exist anywhere in the entire universe except inside of us. You can’t point to it anywhere in the world other than the feelings, thinking, actions, and sometimes even the symptoms you experience in your body.

So, does that mean the fear isn't real? If two people face the same situation, one feels fear and the other doesn't. Does that mean that one of them is making it up?

The fear is not to be confused with the danger. Make no mistake, danger is real. Busy roads are dangerous and cars can kill you. They can kill you if you step out into the road. If you are standing on the road and there is a car coming, you should get out of the way quickly! In the right situation, panic can even be a very appropriate emotion. But that's very different from sitting safely in your house panicking because of the cars out on the road. Experiencing a fear of cars when you are safe inside is an irrational fear. It's not real.

It sounds like a silly statement, but that's what we do when we fear the fear. A healthy concern, sensible caution, a few basic safety procedures, and there would be no need for the emotional response at all. Why use it then? Because we've learned to use it and now the tail is wagging the dog!

If you think about it, if fear is successful in its objective, you avoid the situation you fear and never actually know if the fear was founded in the first place. And because you always experience the fear, you never find out what would happen if you just exercised basic caution without the emotion. The emotion will convince you of its necessity and if you comply, you'll never know any difference. Every time you engage avoidance because of fear, you are reinforcing the credibility of the fear.

The interesting thing about the body's response to fear is that it is exactly the same for an imagined fear as it is an actual fear of something right in front of you in the material world.

If you are in the African Savanna, and you see a lion, your body responds the same whether you actually see a lion or whether you just thought you saw a lion.

If you just think about that, it is amazing. Imagine you are sitting at home staring blankly out the window. Suddenly, just a single thought can pop into your head. Depending on the thought, a feeling of sadness or euphoria or lustfulness or anger can sweep through your body in an instant. Your pancreas secretes a hormone and your liver makes an enzyme that wasn't there just moments before. The blood flow around your body is altered.

And what was the cause of all these physiological changes? A single thought in your mind that doesn't exist anywhere except right there, and only then for a fleeting second.

Bruce Lipton talks about the effects of fear on the body and its ability to perform in a state of stress in his series on Conscious Parenting. He discusses the three key things that happen when we are in a state of fear:

First, the cells of the body move from growth into protection. Blood moves from the viscera at the core of the body out to the extremities (muscles of the arms and legs) in order to engage in 'fight or flight.'

Second, the immune system shuts down because there is no point using energy fighting a virus that may kill you in ten days if this lion could eat you in the next ten seconds.

And third, the blood moves away from the forebrain to the hindbrain so that instead of reason and logic you are better able to engage in reflexive behaviors. You lose your ability to think rationally when you are stressed.

Estimates put the figure at well over 90% for the things we fear but never actually happen. I once heard worry described as chewing gum for the mind — it just gives it something to do but produces no meaningful results.

If a fear of loud noises or a fear of falling is holding you back from reaching your dreams, then you can take comfort in the fact that they've been there all along. But if it's a fear of anything else, then that's something you've picked up along the way. It's something you've learned to see in a certain way, and that means it's something you can unlearn and relearn in a more helpful and healthy way.

Put another way, there are beliefs about the world that you have acquired throughout your life. These beliefs are responsible for the emotions you experience in your body in response to events in the outside world (and your inside world). The feelings you experience in that marvelous body of yours, like doubt, fear, and anxiety, stop you from doing things that you would otherwise like to do. If any of these things are stopping you from achieving your goals and dreams, then the underlying beliefs that are responsible need to go!

ACTION EXERCISES

What are some things that you fear that are preventing you from achieving your dreams?

If those fears have no effect on your goals, don't worry about it, but if they do, what are you willing to do to eradicate that fear or fears?

Is there someone in your past that you must forgive in order to take full responsibility for everything in your life?

Where are you stuck?

Write out the answers or share with a loved-one.

6

DOES EVERYONE SEE IT THAT WAY?

Men are disturbed not by the things that happen to them, but by the views they take of them.

~ Epictetus

I love using the analogy that the inspirational guru Dr. Wayne Dyer used. I ask an audience what would happen if they were to take an orange in their hands and squeeze it really hard? I then ask what would come out of the orange because of their squeezing? Most will either say juice or orange juice. Then I ask the most important question. "Why does orange juice come out?" Some are stumped or try to analyze the physics. Then a genius emerges and says, "Because that's what's inside." The point I make is just that. It's what's inside.

In everyone's life, there are strongly held rules or regulations of, "What ought to be." This is based solely on their own beliefs and experiences. The term is often referred to as a paradigm. When it comes to our reaction to things, it is based on a perception or belief about something, whether that belief is true or not. All of us have probably noticed someone getting really upset about something that occurred, and it's difficult to understand the person's anger or frustration. In most cases, it has nothing to do with what is going on in the situation, but it has everything to do with what's going on inside of them. People tend to react differently in situations all because of their own experiences or what is currently going on inside of them. "It's what's inside."

We are disturbed, not by the events of life, but by the views, we take of them.

~ Epictetus

It is a powerful realization indeed when you understand that your beliefs are the key to your emotions. It is what you believe about the event that causes the emotion, not the event itself.

Our paradigms are very powerful. In 1543, Copernicus revealed on his deathbed that the sun was the center of our universe and not the earth. He knew that his discovery would not be accepted, so he waited until he was dying to reveal the truth. In the early part of the 17th Century, Galileo proved that Copernicus was correct. He spent the rest of his days under house arrest. On May 6th, 1954, Roger Banister broke the four-minute mile. It was believed to be humanly impossible. After he broke the record, many others broke it. What I find so fascinating is that our beliefs get so entrenched in our brain that changing our core beliefs seems crazy. Ralph Waldo Emerson once said, "A foolish consistency is the hobgoblin of little minds."

I once heard a story told that was supposedly true about a man whose wife would always cut the end of the meat when she cooked a pot roast. The husband had never seen this type of culinary art, so he asked his wife why she did it. Her response was that she learned it from her mother. The man happened to be at his mother-in-law's house one day and he asked her the same question. "Mom, why do you cut the ends off the pot roast?" To his surprise, she said, "That's what my mom always did." The man remained unsatisfied, so he went to the grandmother and asked her, "Grandma, why do you cut the ends off your pot roast?" The grandmother clearly exclaimed, "Because it won't fit in the pan."

Your perception of the world is a consequence of your acquired beliefs. And your beliefs are the result of a learning process, not a reflection of reality.

Some people see a situation a certain way and they feel they only have one real option in how to proceed. As a result of this belief, they keep banging their head against the same wall over and over again, going round and round in circles, and getting the same results. But other people see the same situation differently. They perceive a number of different options. They make different choices, and they never experience the same challenges with which the other is stuck.

Choice is a function of awareness.

~ Michael Beckwith

The more aware you are, the more options you perceive in any given situation. The more options brought to your awareness, the higher the likelihood of picking the best option for you in that particular set of circumstances.

This is especially true in relationships. If you allow yourself to continually respond in the same way because you think you are right, then it can perpetuate the same vicious disagreements. You go round and round in angry circles, sometimes for years.

It is not uncommon for people to cling to their sense of rightness, even long after the other party has left or passed away. The same emotions of anger or resentment rise up at the mere thought of the disagreement.

If you can find another way of seeing this — if you can search for other ways to respond — you will eventually bring about a different, better, more healthy result.

And while it may be true that the obligation sits equally with both parties in the relationship, if one just cannot see things differently at the time, and the other can, then the one with the greater awareness has the responsibility for moving things forward.

There is an excellent scene in the movie, Night at the Museum when Ben Stiller's character is hitting the monkey in the face, and the monkey is hitting him back. And on and on it goes for some time. Up rides Teddy Roosevelt on his horse and says, "Larry, why are you hitting the monkey?" He says, "He started it!" And Teddy replies, "Larry, who's evolved?" The responsibility sits with the person with the higher awareness.

Don't bother trying to change the world, the world you see doesn't even exist.

~ Ramana Maharshi

Ramana Maharshi was an Indian mystic who reportedly reached enlightenment at a young age. He said that there are no levels of reality, only levels of experience of the individual. That's a neat way of putting it, isn't it?

He also emphasized the same thing in referring to people's intent on 'saving the world or changing the world' — "Don't bother trying to change the world because the world you see doesn't even exist." Basically, what we can discern from that is the fact that we don't see the world as it is, we see the world as we are.

So how do we gain a higher level of awareness? From experience. But not simply from experience. Everyone gets experience, but not everyone grows at the same rate, do they? The experience must be evaluated in some way and insight needs to be harvested from the experience. That insight needs to lead to a change in the way we see the world and how we operate in it.

Experience is not what happens to a man, it's what a man does with what happens to him.

~ Epictetus

So, you could say that intention mixed with continually evaluated experience leads to a greater level of awareness over time. I love what Swiss psychiatrist, Carl Jung, once said, "Until you make the unconscious conscious, it will direct your life and you will call it fate."

Are you ruled by your emotions? I must be clear in telling you, "Yes, you are!" We all move toward or away from something based on how it makes us feel. So, emotions are the source of all our actions, and those emotions derive from our thoughts and beliefs. But the important question is, "What kinds of emotions are ruling your life?"

When I was a young teenager, my mom bought me a poster that happened to be popular in the early 70's. It had the psychedelic colors and artwork. I really wasn't into that style, but the words on that poster stuck with me forever. Some who read this may remember seeing it. It was a poem called, Desiderata — believed to have been discovered in a Baltimore church in 1692, but the truth was that American writer, Max Ehrmann, (1872–1945), wrote it in 1927. It just so happened that it was discovered in the church that was built in 1692.

I had the poster hanging on the wall in my bedroom. I would frequently read it, until one day I discovered that I had it memorized. I still remember a lot of the words. In fact, a couple of years ago, I was at a friend's office and his secretary had it hanging on the wall beside her desk. I couldn't pass up the opportunity to show off. I said, "Do you see that poem hanging on the wall?" I then turned away from it and started quoting it. She immediately gasped and said that I had a photographic memory. I then revealed the truth and explained to her that I had it on a poster when I was a teen and that I just read it until I committed it to memory. She was still impressed.

There are a couple of phrases in the poem that I'm not impressed with, but the overall poem is meaningful. So, here goes the part that I remember. You may read it in its entirety on the web:

Go placidly amid the noise and the haste, and remember what peace there may be in silence. As far as possible, without surrender, be on good terms with all persons.

Speak your truth quietly and clearly; and listen to others, even to the dull and the ignorant; they too have their story.

Avoid loud and aggressive persons; they are vexatious to the spirit. If you compare yourself with others, you may become vain or bitter, for always there will be greater and lesser persons than yourself.

Enjoy your achievements as well as your plans. Keep interested in your own career, however humble; it is a real possession in the changing fortunes of time.

Exercise caution in your business affairs, for the world is full of trickery. But let this not blind you to what virtue there is; many persons strive for high ideals, and everywhere life is full of heroism.

My main point in telling you about that poem is the fact that I'm confident that it had a huge effect on me. Everything that we've experienced in our lives has been recorded in our brains, and our behaviors are conditioned responses. Neuroscience has proven this. I remember reading one of Dr. Denis Waitley's books where he describes a woman in her 30's undergoing brain surgery while fully awake. When the surgeon touched a certain part of her brain, she relived her 5th birthday party. She remembered by name the friends who were there, the presents she received, and the candles on the cake. She even described the taste of the cake.

Your experiences in life stay with you forever. That can be a challenge for some. But please get this point! What I'm going to tell you is the absolute truth, and the most important message I can give you. You and I have been conditioned by what we have put or allowed to be put into our minds on a regular basis. You've allowed this programming because of your freedom of will. Or, your environment conditioned you. The beauty about what I'm telling you is that you can recondition your mind the same way it was conditioned. You are the captain. You choose success or failure. You choose mediocrity or adventure. You will find what you are looking for whether it's great, bad, or indifferent. Wherever you look, there you are. That is the Law of Correspondence in harmony with the Law of Attraction. Your thoughts radiate out and bring back to you things, people, and circumstances in harmony with your dominant thoughts. "You become what you think about most of the time."

I want to remind you that the only absolute control and freedom you have are the thoughts you think. If you change what goes into your mind, it can and will change your life. For example; the next time you are sitting in traffic daydreaming, thoughts begin to come to you from the subconscious. If any negative thought starts to surface, replace it immediately with a positive affirmation. Get out of your habitual comfort zone.

I want to close this chapter by quoting James Allen. In his book, As a Man Thinketh, there is a quote that resonated with me so much that I memorized it. I quote it to many audiences at the close of my talks. It's about our thoughts and the free will that our Creator has given each of us. Please keep in mind that I will use the term Man to reference humanity, not as gender specific:

Man is either made or unmade by himself. In the armory of thought, he forges the weapons by which he destroys himself. He also fashions the tools with which he builds for himself heavenly mansions of peace, joy, and strength. By the right choice and true application of thought, man can ascend to divine perfection. By the abuse and wrong application of thought, man descends below the level of the beast. Between these two extremes are all the grades of character, and man is their maker and master. Of all the beautiful truths pertaining to the soul, none is more gladdening or fruitful of divine promise and confidence than this; that man is the master of thought, the molder of character, and the maker and shaper of condition, environment, and destiny.

I love James Allen's quote. Even though I don't believe we will ever reach divine perfection in our lives, I'm convinced that with the right thinking, which leads to noble actions, we can leave an awesome legacy.

Change your thoughts and you change your world.

~ Norman Vincent Peale

Co-worker Angela Roach receiving an award from me and her supervisor Spencer Hill

ACTION EXERCISES

What do you feed your mind the first thing in the morning? Is it inspiring? Is it the news? Which should you choose?

Are there certain behaviors that you know do not empower you? Now would be a great time to change that behavior.

What different actions will you commit to doing to replace disempowering ones?

Who can you identify that would be a coach to hold you accountable?

Who sets a great example of a person you admire for behaviors you want to adopt?

Write out the responses. Make a commitment.

7

WE GET WHO WE ARE

Men do not attract what they want, but what they are.

~ James Allen

It's a common theme in motivational and life coaching seminars to hear the advice, "Be the type of person you want to meet." It's good, sound advice, right? It's especially true when we're talking about human relationships. Let's take single people, for example. Do you desire a romantic relationship? Instead of constantly worrying about the type of person you want to meet or eventually marry, it makes much more sense to work on developing yourself into the type of person someone else would want to date or marry.

If you're looking for better opportunities in your career, work on developing a spirit of excellence in all that you do. Work toward making your employer look good instead of trying to make yourself look good.

If this is a new concept to you, welcome to personal development. That's why we call it personal because we are working on ourselves, not others.

But why? Why does it make more sense to cultivate the right inner attitude, motives and heart condition within us instead of worrying about the other person?

I'm glad you asked.

It has to do with the principles and laws of the universe.

I like to use the Bible as a reference point. Let's go back to day three of creation:

"Then God said, Let the earth sprout vegetation, plants yielding seed, and fruit trees on the earth bearing fruit after their kind, with seed in them, and it was so." —Genesis 1:12

I want to pay special attention to the phrase "after their kind." The Greek word for "after their kind" pertains to fruits and vegetables right here, but the phrase itself includes all of creation. The part I want you to understand is that things reproduce "after their kind." Because this is a principle of the universe, it applies to all things. Our thoughts reproduce after their kind. If we are constantly thinking anxiety and fear-based thoughts, they will continue to reproduce building habits or patterns of thinking in our minds that become difficult to break free from. Fear is paralyzing in nature, so when we dwell on fear and allow it into our life, we "get" all the things that go with fear, like anxiety, stress-based illness, skin conditions, and more.

Along with this school of thought is the fact that like attracts like. It is the Law of Attraction. When we operate with a positive attitude, allowing positive thoughts and faith-filled words to permeate the atmosphere around us, we are creating a space for positive things to take place. Our faith puts us in alignment with the promises God has laid out for our lives.

"I know the plans I have for you. Plans to prosper you and not to bring you harm. Plans to give you a hope and a future." —Jeremiah 29:11

But we don't just magically get the promises of God flowing in our life. We have to grab hold of them. We do this by believing them. That's called faith, and faith in action will attract all of God's goodness toward us. I recommend that you read the book of James in the New Testament. As John Maxwell once said, "It's a book that you really need to read standing up." As the Apostle James said, "Faith without works is dead." When faith is put to action, it moves you from a belief to a knowing.

Do you see how it works?

I want to mention another quote from the outstanding book, As a Man Thinketh. "The soul attracts that which it secretly harbors, that which it loves, and also that which it fears. It reaches the height of its cherished aspirations. It falls to the level of its unchastened desires —

and circumstances are the means by which the soul receives its own."

What a profound description of the human condition and the way we are wired. We, in this life, will not get what we want, but instead, we will get what we are inside. Like the orange, when it has been squeezed reveals the juice inside, so are we. The thoughts, fears, and desires we secretly harbor in our soul eventually come out. The Bible says, "Every hidden thing shall be revealed."

So, why am I telling you all this? What is the solution? I mean, for those of us who aren't always thinking the best, most honorable thoughts, this can be quite problematic.

It is the height of all ignorance to ignore the fact that thoughts become things. The solution is to change the way we think. Remember that the only thing that you have total control over are the thoughts that you think on a regular basis, and right thinking can easily begin with the words we say to ourselves.

I once heard Zig Ziglar humorously say once that contrary to what you have ever been told, it is okay to talk to yourself. He went on to say that it's also okay to even answer yourself, but when your start to say, "huh?" to the answer, you may have a problem.

The next time you sit quietly with no distractions, examine your thoughts. Some of those habitual 60,000 thoughts will start to emerge from your subconscious. Once you're conscious of the fact that some of those thoughts are becoming negative, that's where you have total control to change them. You can use your very own command of positive affirmations and words that empower you. "Yes, start talking to yourself."

"Pleasant words are as a honeycomb, sweet to the soul and health to the bones."
— Proverbs 16:24

The words we use have power. They can make us laugh or cry. They can wound or heal. They offer us hope or devastation. With words, we can make our noblest intentions felt and our deepest desires known. In fact, the English language has far more words to describe emotions than any other language. All of us have probably heard the old saying, "Sticks and stones can break my bones, but words can never hurt me." What a lie that is! The truth is, words can hurt far more than sticks and stones. The words we say to ourselves, whether spoken silently or aloud, do have consequences.

Choose your words carefully. The next time someone asks you, "How are you doing today," be ready to unleash something powerful. There are only a few responses that I use when I'm asked that question. I will only say the following: Great! Outstanding! Wonderful! Wonderfully blessed! Or, if I'm with others who know me well, I'll even say, "Man, if I were doing any better, I'd have to sit on my hands to keep from clapping!" You may find what I'm telling you to be silly, but I know for a fact that it worked for me, and it's worked for all who've made it a habit.

When you say positive affirmations, your mind will attract positive experiences. The words you say create feelings and those feelings give off vibrational frequencies that will correspond with other like frequencies. Thought waves do travel like sound waves, only much faster. Make it a new empowering habit. Remember, we are creatures of habit. It could take you up to a month to get it right. I once heard Denis Waitley say that habits start off like flimsy cobwebs, and with practice, they become unbreakable steel cables that either shackle or strengthen your life.

We aren't even aware of most habitual words and actions that we say and do. We've become masters of our habits. When our habits are formed, we've become unconsciously competent in the task. We don't even need to use our conscious thoughts to perform the acts.

I wish I could discover who came up with the four levels of mastery, or the four levels of learning. If someone should happen upon the genius who did, please give him or her credit for it, and let me know who it was. Here are the four:

1. Unconscious Incompetence
2. Conscious Incompetence
3. Conscious Competence
4. Unconscious Competence (Mastery)

Let me illustrate how this works. I'll use shoe tying as an example.

A baby at birth can't tie its shoe. It doesn't even know that the skill exists. Therefore, it is at level one, (unconscious incompetence). At about the age of two, the baby observes its mommy or daddy tying its shoe. So, it knows the skill exists, but it can't perform the task, (conscious incompetence). Then, the baby grows to the age of around four or five, and mommy or daddy has taught the skill to their son or daughter. The child may struggle to get it right, and it still must think about it. You may sometimes even watch the child sticking out its tongue, or hear it saying 'left over right', but the skill was learned and thinking must be in the equation, (conscious competence). When the child matures to its teen years, he or she doesn't have to think about the task in any detail. He or she just ties the shoe, (unconscious competence).

Our habits of thought are exactly the same. The unconscious or subconscious directs our pathway to success and happiness or failure and misery. I know that that's a hard pill for some to swallow. At the reading of what I just mentioned, some will say, "I don't want to live the way, think the way, or feel the way I'm feeling! Randy Perdue, you are nuts!" Well, I'm here to tell you, "Yes, you are responsible!" You can continue to stay bitter and blame God, the universe, your spouse, your parents, etc., or you can get out of the comfort zone and create new thoughts, words, feelings, and actions.

One of my mentors of the John Maxwell Team, Christian Simpson, once said that the majority are walking around in a state of unconsciousness. He said that they were basically sleepwalking. What he meant by that is that the majority are ruled by the typical thoughts they have day-to-day. They never take advantage of conscious thought and controlling those thoughts.

Now that you have this awareness, the next time you are sitting in a traffic jam or waiting for the traffic light to change, pay attention to the thoughts that surface. Be ready to go on the attack with any negative thoughts that attempt to creep in and take over. Whatever you focus on will expand. A negative thought is attracted to another negative thought. It's like the thought has tentacles that reach out and grab hold of other similar thoughts. Before you know it, an army of negative soldiers that defend its turf rules your conscious mind. Then, those thoughts begin to control your feelings.

Those feelings give off an electrical vibration or frequency that activate the Law of Attraction. Ultimately, guess what shows up in your environment? I think you get it.

In 1986, Dr. Shad Helmstetter wrote an excellent book called, What to Say When You Talk to Yourself. I find it most amazing that the latest discovery in neuroscience proves that we have the power to modify our brain activity and create new neuro-networks. In the study of neuroplasticity, it's been proven that we can alter the pathways of our brains by repeated thoughts and words we say to ourselves. In other words, we can change our lives by the thoughts and words we use on a regular basis. We are not stuck!

Remember this — everything begins with the thoughts we think. When we change our thoughts, we change our world. Our new thoughts can literally recreate us!

James Allen spoke of the seed reproducing after its kind when he said that a man's character was the complete sum of his thoughts, "As the plant springs from and could not be without the seed, so every act of a man springs from the hidden seed of thought, and could not have appeared without them. This applies equally to those acts called spontaneous and unpremeditated as to those which are deliberately executed."

Bottom line? Our lives cannot hide from our thoughts. They are like seeds that will grow and produce. It's both wonderful and terrifying to think that the sum of our thoughts will be (and already are) revealed in our lives. Wow!

As you continue to walk in awareness, living in agreement both outwardly and inwardly becomes increasingly important.

You hold the key to every situation in your life, and you have the power to build your life by choosing the right thoughts. There is no element of chance, but there is the opportunity to turn around any situation by first taking control of your thought life.

The Bible tells us to "take every thought captive." We are not supposed to just allow our mind to be a playground or a movie screen with unmonitored activity going on 24/7. We have to take control of the scenes we choose to watch.

By choosing wisely, our tomorrow can look like whatever we decide. Are you ready to start guarding your thoughts?

If you think you are beaten, you are;
If you think you dare not, you don't.
If you'd like to win, but you think you can't,
It is almost a cinch that you won't.
If you think you'll lose, you're lost;
For out of the world we find
Success begins with a fellow's will
It's all in the state of mind.
If you think you're outclassed, you are;
You've got to think high to rise.
You've got to be sure of yourself before
You can ever win the prize.
Life's battles don't always go
To the stronger or faster man;
But sooner or later the man who wins
Is the one who thinks he can!

~ Walter D. Wintle

ACTION EXERCISES

Begin by asking empowering questions the next time a situation or condition causes negative thoughts or actions to occur.

Questions like:

What is the lesson here?

What's good about what I'm feeling or experiencing?

Right now, I am grateful for what?

How can I take this crisis and turn it into an opportunity?

Statements to say when the ugly head of negativity should begin to enter your mind:

I am wonderfully blessed!

I am God's greatest earthly miracle!

I am living a life of purpose and meaning!

8

ARE YOU MILKING THIS?

Every action has its pleasures and its price.

~ Socrates

Have you witnessed a person who had a misfortunate accident, which left them handicapped in some physical way, and yet they have such a marvelous attitude? In fact, it appeared that the accident was a blessing, and they were much better off than they were before the accident. Conversely, what about the ones you know who have so many opportunities, and have wonderful health and prosperity, yet every time you engage in any dialog with them, the sky is always falling, — the glass is half empty? Sure, we all encounter this unusual behavior.

It seems that some are not satisfied in having a discussion unless they get to complain about something. I have very little patience with that type of conversation. In fact, I used to tell my secretary, Fay Walker, to do my caring for me. She laughed because she knew how I actually felt. Please don't misunderstand me. I know that there are those who have serious issues and require professional treatment. I'm not including those who are suffering and require medication. I'm speaking of those who have absolutely nothing physically or mentally wrong but rely on habitual whining.

The 'poor me' syndrome (as it were) occurs during the moment when the person first realizes there is a definite benefit in sharing the story of how unfortunate they've been in order to receive attention and sympathy. Being a victim can have good payoffs, after all. It also excuses them from the effort of trying, doesn't it?

To illustrate this phenomenon in human behavior, I found a most interesting story about U.S. President William McKinley (1897-1901). He was the 25th President, as well as one of four U.S. Presidents assassinated while serving as President. His wife and First Lady, Ida Saxton McKinley, was a frail woman according to reports, and she would begin to feel ill when President McKinley had important guests or cabinet meetings. She would complain so tenaciously that the President would have to lie in the bed next to her — holding her to provide her with the comfort and attention she required. He would then have to reschedule his engagements. I can only speculate as to the reasons behind her behavior, but the fact that the McKinley's daughters died at a very young age may have something to do with it.

Do you ever wonder how people survived without antidepressants? I find that the use of antidepressants in America is alarming, as is the administering of drugs to children with the ADHD or ADD syndrome. As Simon Sinek points out in his book, Leaders Eat Last, he feels that there is a distraction addition, not ADD or ADHD. We stimulate our children with all the latest technology, then place them in a traditional classroom and expect them to be still and quiet. We have gradually progressed into an age where drugs are the answer.

I like to refer to this epidemic as, "The boiling frog syndrome." If you drop a frog into hot water, it will immediately jump out. However, if you put a frog into water that is at room temperature, then turn up the heat, it will lie in the water and eventually boil to death. The frog adjusts to the gradual climb in temperature. Are we experiencing something similar? Are we being desensitized to the conditions in our environment because of the subtle changes? Let's look at some facts.

In the 1950's few of us went to weekly sessions with a therapist. Today, according to the Hoover Institute there are currently…

- 77,000 clinical psychologist
- 192,000 clinical social workers
- 105,000 mental health counselors

- 50,000 marriage and family therapist
- 17,000 nurse psychotherapist
- 30,000 life coaches

Of course, by sharing this truth with some might get them upset with me. I do find it amazing that many seem to be fulfilled when they constantly complain, then they're off to see the doctor to get some pills to feel better. Nevertheless, it must be acknowledged that there are often benefits to others proclaimed misery.

I read where a psychoanalyst uses a unique line of questioning. Whenever anyone first explains their problems to him, the very first question he asks himself is how convenient is this? In other words, what are you getting out of this?

Dr. David Hawkins recommended putting a sign up on the mirror where you could see it every morning that reads, "Yours is the saddest story I've ever heard!"

Dr. David Fink, a psychiatrist with the Veterans Administration, wrote an article in Coronet Magazine entitled, Release Form Nervous

Tension. In the article, Dr. Fink describes his research of over 10,000 patients who suffered from severe tension – those who had psychological imbalances. What he found most interesting is that all of his patients were habitual faultfinders. His conclusions were that the habit of fault-finding is the prelude or mark of the mentally unbalanced.

There are two types of people in the world, aren't there? There are life giving people and life draining people. Life-giving people add value. They leave you a little bit better than you were when they found you. They tend to see the world from your perspective with you.

We don't build up or encourage people by telling them how great we are; we build them up or encourage them by telling them how great they are.

You may have heard the story of the lady who went to dinner with Mr. Gladstone one evening and Mr. Disraeli, both prominent English Statesman. She said, "After dinner with Mr. Gladstone, I thought he was the smartest person in England, but after dinner with Mr. Disraeli, I thought I was!"

What a difference between the two! Life-giving people make you feel better about yourself, but they also make you feel better about the world and everyone in it. They seem to lift everything and leave you with hope. You always feel better leaving the company of a life-giving person.

Life draining people, on the other hand, tend to talk about themselves, and they see the world from their perspective. You always feel worse when leaving the company of life draining people!

Most of us are not aware of our real motivations. A wealthy person can work hard, make money and declare that she is doing it for the family. But the family never sees her, and when they do she seems angry. They feel like they can't live up to her high expectations. They feel like a disappointment to her. Is she really doing it for the family? Is it possible there are hidden motives? She loves the attention and the respect. Maybe she enjoys not having to look after her own children.

On the other side of the coin, a person could be without a job, and because of a lack of finances, he or she might be forced to live on state benefits. Suffering at home all day with not enough money for some fancy car, expensive clothes, or holidays to exotic places doesn't bother some, but how convenient could that be? If you don't have a job, you don't have to go in every day!

Of course, these are simple examples not meant to be illustrative of EVERYONE in those situations, but it is certainly true that the truth is seldom in the appearance of things. In order to move up and move on, we have to let go. If you are going to be mentally and emotionally healthy, you need to let go of the opportunities you have to continually seek pity and sympathy from everyone you meet! If you really want to have a great family life, you need to make it a priority and stop doing all the other things that prevent you from sharing experiences and making memories with your family. If you really want a job, you need to let go of all the upsides of not working and spend your time learning how to become a better job candidate.

Some of you, as you read through this chapter, will be offended at the mere suggestion that your misery has any upside whatsoever. How horrible of me to even come up with such an outlandish idea! And then you will seek out people to validate your feelings. You'll tell them how offended you are. And you will explain again just how awful your lot in life is. Once again, you will soak up whatever sympathy is available.

In one of Paul Martinelli's incredible teaching, he describes the tendency of people to look for opportunities to be offended as one of the four pillars of drama. Why would anyone possibly look to be offended? Simply because there is something in it for them.

Perhaps this is why Socrates said, "Know thyself." The unexamined life is not worth living. If you are really honest with yourself, how convenient are your challenges? Are you prepared to give up these conveniences in order to move forward with your life?

I was recently on a teaching call with John Maxwell when he said, "Attitude is not the only thing, but it is the main thing." Having the right attitude is not only essential, it's foundational. Whining and complaining will keep you stuck.

Taking on the attitude of gratitude will change your life significantly.

One of the best ways to recondition your attitude is to make a gratitude list. A few years ago, I wrote the top 100 things in my life that made me grateful. I knew that it was important to write that list when I was totally alone, and it was important to write within the first thirty minutes upon awakening in the morning. Famous American Author, Henry Ward Beecher, called it the rudder of the day. Your subconscious mind is more amenable to your suggestions upon awakening.

The next time you catch yourself starting to complain about anything, catch yourself, and replace that internal dialog with a phrase like, "I am grateful for the lesson that this situation is teaching me." Or, something simple like, "I am wonderfully blessed." What you speak about — you bring about, whether you say it aloud or silently to yourself. The subconscious reacts without judgment or bias.

"Neurotics complain of their illness, but they make the most of it, and when it comes to taking it away from them they will defend it like a lioness her young."

~ Sigmund Freud

ACTION EXERCISES

Where are you stuck in your life?

Do you find excuses as to why you are stuck?

Ask a friend or loved-one if they feel that you complain often.

Catch yourself the next time you have an urge to complain about anything. Make it a 24-hour exercise. You will notice a difference.

Avoid conversations with others who are complainers. You may have to take a leave of absence for a day to accomplish this task.

9

YOU ARE PERFECT JUST AS YOU ARE!

Be kind for everyone you meet is fighting a hard battle.

~ Socrates

I've been blessed to have had the opportunity to do a lot of traveling to numerous countries in my lifetime. One of the things that I've learned is that regardless of the culture, everyone is the same in many ways. Everyone wants to be happy and healthy. They want and need to love and to be loved, and most aspire to have a better life and live a life of purpose and meaning.

I believe we are all perfectly imperfect, created by God to live significant lives. No matter where you go or to whom you speak, everyone is stepping forward courageously to face the human condition. The courage of a mother to risk her life to give birth to another life, or the courage of a father to stand up to protect his family, his country, his way of life to include the courage of every single one of us to stand up and say yes to our life experience.

We are not all meant to be star quarterbacks, nor beauty pageant queens. We are not all meant to be president or Mother Teresa.

What I find so fascinating is the fact that many of us were indoctrinated in the belief that our success will be determined by our Intelligence Quotient or IQ. I'm sure that you can remember those who were superstars academically and turned out to be dismal failures. Scientific evidence as well as sophisticated statistics have clearly debunked that paradigm. In fact, only six percent of entrepreneurial success (in other words, the rich) is attributed to IQ and up to forty-five percent of success is due to EQ or Emotional Intelligence.

Please understand that I'm not totally bashing our education system, but let me ask you a question. Did you ever take a class in high school or college on "Success?" Why are there so many MBA graduates unemployed or bankrupt? Science now proves that there are other measurements of intelligence. IQ identifies with analytical, logical, technical, and rational abilities. EQ identifies with self-awareness, self-expression, people skills, decision making, and how one deals with stress and change. There is also physical intelligence and spiritual intelligence. IQ is the least quantifiable indicator of success.

Moms and Dads, don't worry about your kids if they have a lot of street smarts and people skills, but bring home a "C" or worse from time to time. Just read the statistics, and I'm confident you'll come to the same conclusion many others have reached.

For those who have dedicated themselves to a career of academia, I applaud you for a life committed to education. I do strongly encourage you to explore the research I've described. For many decades, we have been taught what to think and not how to think. The fact that scholastic indicators such as the SAT and ACT are inept in determining success should be eye opening for you. We should never tell children and young adults that having a three digit IQ is a must for success in life. It is misleading and it plants the seeds of failure in their minds. I personally know two high school dropouts who are millionaires. One of whom made ten million dollars in a single year. I would be wise to emphasize that having a lot of money is only an indicator of success. It is not the only indicator of a successful life. If money becomes your God, you are in big trouble. I merely point this out for the purpose of changing perspectives of how intelligence is measured.

Every single one of us is different, and every single one of us is a miracle. Each one struggles in some area of life, and every single one of us is loved by someone, and unconditionally loved by our Creator.

If you look around, you see people doing their best. Most are doing the best they can with what they know. The problem lies in the fact that many do not know what's for their own good. Everyone makes the best decision they can at the time with what they know.

If we accept the fact that we do what we do because we don't know any better, then our path becomes pretty straightforward, doesn't it?

How can we learn more and grow more so that we can make better decisions? How can we be just a little more enlightened?

Paul Martinelli often says, "The perfect curriculum for your growth is whatever lies in front of you right now." I find this a very empowering train of thought.

We are all perfectly imperfect.

No one is any better than anyone else.

No one is any worse than anyone else.

We are all doing the best we can.

We can all do better.

We all have the opportunity to learn and grow.

As we learn and grow we make better decisions.

As we make better decisions our lives improve.

Isn't it nice to think that we are ALL doing the best we can? It certainly makes pride seem pretty empty and forgiveness much more of a rational decision. "Forgive us our trespasses as we forgive those that trespass against us."

Forgiveness is the fragrance the violet sheds on the heel that has crushed it.

~ Mark Twain

There is a story about the word Ubuntu, which, to a certain African tribe means, "I am what I am because of who we all are."

It is said that an anthropologist who was studying the customs and lifestyle of this tribe spent a lot of time with the children. One particular day he decided to play a game with them. He knew they loved candy, so he made a trip to a neighboring town to buy some. He arranged quite a few pieces in a decorative basket and placed the prize at the base of a tree.

Excitedly, he called all the children together explaining that they were going to play a game, and the winner would receive the prize, "When I shout 'now', everyone will run as fast as you can to the tree! The first one there wins the entire basket of candy."

Eager to participate, the children lined up and waited for the shout. As soon as the anthropologist yelled, "Now!" all the children grabbed each other by the hand and began running as fast as they could toward the tree. Arriving at exactly the same time, they divided the candy and began to enjoy their prize.

Slightly stunned, the anthropologist asked why they chose to all run together when the winner would have had all the candy to himself.

Ubuntu! "How could one of us be happy when the others are sad?"

This philosophy and way of life speak about our interconnectedness. You can't exist as a human all by yourself. Our choices affect others. Every day we have crossroads and decisions. With each decision, we either choose to add value to another human life or to take it away. We are always choosing one or the other. Even the decision to do nothing is still a decision.

Part of walking in awareness is understanding that we are responsible for the condition in which we leave others. How has their encounter with us affected them? What lasting impression have I left?

We often talk about leaving a legacy for future generations. Often, we are referring to finances or inheritance, but what about our daily legacy? We are building a memorial to ourselves with every sentence, every text message, every email, every glance. Realizing this certainly changes our perspective, doesn't it?

Please reflect on what I mentioned about intelligence on page 125 as you read the following quotes from some pretty sharp individuals:

Education consists mainly of what we've unlearned.

~ Mark Twain

Education is what happens when one has forgotten everything he learned in school.

~ Albert Einstein

It is possible to store the mind with a million facts and still be entirely uneducated.

~ Alec Bourne

ACTION EXERCISES

With what aspects of your life, thoughts, attitude, or actions are you not happy?

How do those aspects affect your life?

Do you know anyone who has the same challenges as you do, but doesn't let those challenges bother him or her or uses them as an advantage?

How could it be true that your weaknesses are not significant enough to sabotage your success?

Do you give too much attention to your weaknesses and not enough attention to your strengths?

Write out the answers, or think about them, or better yet, discuss them with a loved one.

10

LOVE ALL LIFE, INCLUDING YOURSELF!

There are two basic motivating forces; fear and love. When we are afraid, we pull back from life. When we love, we open to all that life has to offer with passion, excitement, and acceptance. We need to learn to love ourselves first, in all our glory and imperfections. If we cannot love ourselves, we cannot fully open our ability to love others or our potential to create.

~ John Lennon

Christ said, "Love thy neighbor as thyself." I believe Him, don't you? I believe that it's impossible to love another human being without first loving yourself. I'm not talking about being narcissistic or conceited. I'm talking about a healthy self-esteem and self-concept. As Zig Ziglar once quoted, "God don't make no junk." If you don't love yourself, how can you give to others something that you don't have inside? It just can't flow to others if it doesn't flow in you.

You have flaws. I have flaws. We are not perfect. We're all going to make mistakes. It's simply part of the human process. Shocking, right?

I'm quite certain you didn't flinch at all when you read those words. Isn't it amazing that although we are fully aware of the fact that mistakes, detours, and unexpected results are all part of the process, we often allow the fear of their arrival to stall our progress? Some of us get stuck for days or weeks, while others struggle with the fear of failure to such a degree that it can derail our dreams indefinitely. But why? Why do we get stuck?

In the closing chapters of Think and Grow Rich, Napoleon Hill uncovers the six basic fears that prevent us from attaining freedom and success:

- The fear of poverty.

- The fear of criticism.
- The fear of ill health.
- The fear of losing someone.
- The fear of old age.
- The fear of death.

These are core fears. As we talked about earlier, they are learned. Depending on how we were raised or what we've experienced, these fears can affect us to a greater or lesser degree.

How do we combat fear? How do we push past the irrational and negative thought patterns that trigger survival mode and constrict the hope around us? How do we live struggle free?

The good news is that there is a way to retrain your brain. It doesn't matter if you're eighteen or eighty, the negative thoughts that run through your brain can be recognized, rejected, and replaced.

Let's take a look at how that's accomplished:

Fear is connected to our lens. It has to do with how we see things, and especially, how we see ourselves. For the most part, we see situations through our own filter or according to certain expectations. We do this automatically, or without really thinking about it.

For example, let's say five or six of us were discussing real estate investing during dinner. The deeper a few of us got into the conversation, the more you checked-out and disengaged. Why did you check-out? It's because you're not an investor, so you mentally dismissed yourself from the conversation.

Not only do you not invest in real estate, but also you've never owned a home in your life. In fact, your parents never owned a home either. So, instead of leaning in (which would be alignment), you might choose to lean away. It probably wasn't even a conscious decision. You see, the left side of our brain (the part that's linear and rational) is constantly taking information from our experiences and connecting this information to our current reality in order to project probable outcomes. So, if the entire table is talking about investing and you don't believe that's something attainable for you, it's likely the left side of your brain made the probable assumption that you'll never need this information, so go ahead and checkout.

Hold it right there!

What if investing becomes somehow connected to your future success? What if you're a late bloomer but buying property is now vital to your life? Well, once you have this awareness (become awake to this truth) you have the power to change, to learn, to grow.

Maybe you'll have to overcome some of the core fears Napoleon Hill discussed. Fear robs us of our power. While we are saying yes to our dreams and goals, fear is saying no.

Instead of allowing these fears to run around in our brain like a wild banshee, it's up to us to……

RECOGNIZE them,

REJECT them, and

REPLACE them.

It's like being the bouncer of your own brain. If there are negative thoughts and limiting belief systems in there, it's our job to kick them out!

Let's go one level deeper and talk about how we kick negative thoughts out. It's certainly not by using willpower and choosing not to think negative thoughts. If you've ever attempted to not think about something, you know how well that works.

If you've never tried it, go ahead and spend the next thirty seconds trying not to picture a purple elephant. Don't do it! No purple elephants!

Let me guess … they're walking around in your brain in full color, right? I thought so. Instead of attempting to not think negatively, the key is to replace fear and negative thoughts. We do this by reminding ourselves of who we are, what we're made of, and what's available to us.

You can use any positive affirmations you choose. The only requirement is that you believe what you're reading or declaring.

Simple Bible Scriptures can be very useful. They can act as your Daily Promises.

Here are a few:

Trust in the Lord with all your heart, and lean not on your own understanding. In all your ways acknowledge Him, and He shall direct your paths. —Proverbs 3: 5-6

Finally, brethren, whatever things are true, whatever things are noble, whatever things are just, whatever things are pure, whatever things are lovely, whatever things are of good report, if there is any virtue, and if there is anything praiseworthy-meditate on these things. —Philippians 4:8

And we know that all things work together for good to those who love God, to those who are the called according to His purpose. —Romans 8:28

These are just a few, but you get the point. Replace the lies fear is trying to tell you with the truth of who you really are! When your thought-life is centered around faith and truth, you become a living, breathing, container of hope. You actually begin to operate on a higher vibrational level. You begin to attract the things you desire because you aren't allowing any interference from fear!

I believe it's possible to form the habit of walking free from fear. It may take some practice, but the ability to boldly embrace who we are and live an authentic, courageous life is possible. Remember, failure isn't fatal, and it certainly isn't final.

So go ahead and do it! Whether you fail or not, at least you are busy with living instead of standing on the sidelines of life, and that's something to be applauded!

In 2012, Sara Blakely became the youngest self-made billionaire. She was 41. She is the creator and founder of Spanx, a women's apparel product. The thing that was impressive about her story was her recollection of sitting around the dinner table with her father every evening. He taught her the power of failing big and failing often. "Every evening he would ask me, 'so, what did you fail at today?' And if there were no failures, Dad would be disappointed."

Lack of failure means you are not stretching yourself outside your comfort zone.

By focusing on failing often, and using it as a freeing and liberating exercise in the process of becoming, Sara was allowed to understand that a lack of failure actually signified that she was not stretching herself far enough out of her comfort zone.

Each day we should strive to fully embrace life and all the mess that it may bring. It's when we live to be more than we were yesterday, and chase after it without fear, that we can begin to discover what we are made of and what we can become!

A large percentage of our society always plays it safe. Something inside of them is dissatisfied, but failing is so uncomfortable. Thomas Edison discovered over 10,000 ways that the light bulb wouldn't work. What if he stopped at 1000? Would we still be living with kerosene lit lamps? Science journals called Edison a quack. Abraham Lincoln failed in public office eight times before ever being elected as President. He suffered from depression for losing his first true love, Ann Rutledge. He went on to become the United States 16th President, and probably the most beloved President ever.

I love the following quote by President Teddy Roosevelt. It should inspire anyone who is ready to step out of the comfort zone:

It is not the critic who counts, not the man who points out how the strong man stumbles, or when the doer of deeds could have done them better. The credit belongs to the man in the arena, whose face is marred by dust and sweat and blood, who strives valiantly — who knows the great enthusiasms, the great devotions, who spends himself in a worthy cause, who at the best knows in the end the triumph of high achievement, and who at the worst, if he fails, at least fails while daring greatly, so that his place shall never be with those cold and timid souls who have known neither victory or defeat!

~ Teddy Roosevelt

I encourage you to take risks — push against the imaginary barriers of life. Swim in the deep end! Choose to free-fall! Don't worry about failing. If you fail, it's really okay! You'll get up. You'll try again! You'll make it!

It took me 15 years to work out I had no talent for writing, but I couldn't give it up because by then I was too famous!

~Robert Benchley

ACTION EXERCISES

Who do you need to forgive?

Why don't you forgive them?

Where have you made mistakes in your own life?

Why is it so hard for you to forgive yourself?

Plunge Takers

Training Directors for Departments of Corrections at Arora, CO

Symposium in 2015

National Institute of Corrections

Left to Right:

VA-Joe Bridge, Ohio-Dr. Tracy Reveal, WV-Yours Truly, NV-Gary Rosenfeld. PA-Mike Dooley, Iowa- Trish Signor, NE-Ken Sturdy (The God Father) OR- Jeanine Hohn, Philadelphia PA-Edwin Cruz

11

IF IT'S WORTH HAVING IT'S HARD TO GET!

I can sum up the success of my life in seven words. Never give up. Never, never give up.

~ Winston Churchill

The spark is fun, isn't it? It's that moment of creation when you give permission to a dream or a goal. That spark is usually accompanied by feelings of determination, optimism, passion and motivation. Beginnings are exciting and energizing. They have the freshness of a blank page, and for most people, a new endeavor can be almost intoxicating. It's kind of like the honeymoon phase of a relationship. And just like romantic relationships, substance isn't built in the beginning. It's during the trials and the day-to-day encounters with each other that 'who we are inside' is established. It's when we are faced with difficult choices, challenges, trials and frustrations that we become.

During this process of becoming, our dreams are either being fulfilled or forgotten. It happens one choice at a time because it is the process that builds us into who we really are.

Success is developed daily, not in a day.

Look around at your life. Think about your relationships, finances, and career. Now go deeper. Think about the things that make you proud, the things for which you've settled, and the things you'd like to change.

Everything around you is a manifestation of your daily choices. You are currently in the active possession of the kingdom you've created for yourself. Good or bad — like it or not — you are the product of your choices.

The more I meditate on this, the more I realize that there is an art to living out our passion. It is an ebb and flow, a process of constant evolving and adapting.

If you aren't happy with what you currently have, the answer then is to begin to lean-in to the choices that say yes to the fulfillment of your dreams and goals. In order to accomplish this, there really is a leveling of pride that takes place. In order to grow and become all that you can be, you'll need to first take responsibility for who and WHERE you are.

Nothing good was ever born out of excuses, so if you've ever said things like, "This is how I was raised," or "I can't help it — I'm just doing what I know." I want to challenge you to absolutely ban these excuses from your life. You don't have to remain comfortable with terrible circumstances. You can take the sign off your bathroom mirror because yours doesn't have to be the saddest story ever, but it's up to you to make that decision. Living your best life is your own choice.

It is one of the most liberating things you'll ever do. To stand on the wreckage heap of your own broken promises, unfulfilled commitments, lies, masks, failures, and mistakes and place your signature of ownership on the whole mess; that's huge! It gives you a starting point, a place of accountability where you can say, "Yes, I'm responsible for all of that, and now I'm going to be responsible for all of this!"

That thought process is better than skydiving for the first time. It's risky, dangerous, wildly vulnerable, and 100% necessary if things are ever going to be any different in your life. Best of all, it's empowering.

We are who we choose to be. Every day. Every moment.

We don't have to wait until church on Sunday or even tomorrow morning. We literally have the power to walk in foolishness one minute and turn our entire life around the next. As soon as we realize we are doing something that's not in alignment with our best life, we have the power to choose to turn around. That decision can be made in an instant.

Right now. Or right now. Or right now!

Any moment is the right moment to adjust your alignment. And once you decide, you give permission once again to the fulfillment of your dream, your goal, and your purpose.

And how do my tiny choices have anything to do with what level of success I'm able to attain (and maintain) in my life?

I'm glad you asked.

Star athletes don't become champions in the ring or on the field — they are merely recognized there.

Success is merely the evidence of the level of discipline and commitment you've held up. It's just like physical muscles are proof of your commitment to work out every day.

We become champions every time we say yes to our dream, get up early, finished our workout routine, and do what others are not willing to do in order to better themselves. Our success or failure is hidden in our daily routine. That's where it all happens. If we cheat there, it will come out eventually.

Former heavyweight champion, Joe Frazier, said, "You can map out a fight plan, but when the action starts, it boils down to reflexes. That's where your roadwork shows. If you've cheated on that in the dark of the morning, you'll get found out under the bright lights."

This is a perfect analogy for success in every area of our lives. It's all about what you do when no one is watching. It's about what you do to prepare. Do you walk in excellence? Do you operate in integrity? Are all of your choices bringing you closer to the fulfillment of your dream?

Okay, now let's go back to the chapter title, "If it's worth having, it's hard to get." This statement is both true and untrue at the same time. The bottom line is this; any choice you make has 'hard' attached to it.

Choice #1: If you choose to live with intention and fulfill your destiny, it will be hard. Things will come against you. You'll often have to go against the status quo. You may feel lonely at times and without encouragement. You'll need self-discipline, commitment, and to constantly remind yourself that you can do this. You'll have to give yourself pep-talks and learn how to quickly realign yourself when you start to drift off course. Are all these things hard? Absolutely!

Choice #2: If you choose to slack off, settle for less than you are capable of or become complacent, it will be hard. You'll constantly wonder what you could have achieved if you had only changed your habits and said yes to your dreams. You'll regret the fact that you never stepped out of your comfort zone long enough to experience the thrill of success. It will be hard to look at your life one day and wonder what you could have been if only you would have given yourself permission.

If you look at it this way, I'm sure you'll agree that both choices are hard. It's just that one comes with the promise of a fulfilled life and the ability to walk in freedom, while the other comes with disappointment and regret. We either pay the price for failing to pursue our passions, or we enjoy the price we paid for success through perseverance.

The greatest oak was once just a little nut who held its ground.

~Anonymous

ACTION EXERCISES

What is the difference between being stubborn and being committed?

When you give up on something, how do you explain it to yourself? Do you identify good reasons why you are stopping?

What is the upside of giving up in these areas?

What is the downside of giving up in these areas?

Write out the answers, or think about them, or better yet, discuss them with a loved one.

12

WHERE IS MY WHY?

The two most important days of your life are the day you were born, and the day you find out why.

~ Mark Twain

Each one of us was created with a purpose. There is an internal version of yourself, fully equipped with unique gifts, talents, and passions. This true version of yourself can either be suppressed, starved and ignored or nurtured and given the freedom to grow. The choice is yours.

You're not a carbon copy of anyone else. If you were, you'd be dispensable. Anyone could fill your shoes and your purpose in life. But they absolutely cannot.

We complicate things, don't we? I think the fact that we are thinking and reasoning adults are sometimes our downfall, especially when it comes to finding our 'why.' We start out as children filled with wonder and optimism. Children say things like, "I want to fly. I want to touch the stars. I want to live under water." Their sense of having the ability to become whatever they want has no boundaries. Limitations are learned later in life. As parents, it's our job to nurture our children's dreams and encourage them to follow their natural path. There are numerous childhood development studies that outline the benefits of allowing your child to search, explore, and follow their dreams.

The Bible provides some awe-inspiring insight into this way of thinking. Proverbs 18:16 assures us, "A man's gifts will make room for him."

Your gift is that divine spark that was planted in you at birth. It is that certain something you were created to live out and be. Your gift is connected to your purpose, your passion and ultimately, your ability to live a fulfilled life. It is all wrapped up in your big 'why.'

When you're operating in your gift and walking out your purpose, it doesn't matter how difficult the journey is. It doesn't matter how much time it takes to evolve or become exactly what you are called to be. Money, education, and time invested in your purpose don't feel like a sacrifice to you because it's what you are meant to do! There is an inner passion connected to our purpose!

German philosopher Friedrich Nietzsche said, "He who has a why to live for can bear almost any how."

How long? How difficult? How much will it cost me? How far will I have to go? How much more will I have to learn? How many more obstacles will I face? These things don't matter when you have your 'why!'

It's interesting to take note of the fact that the Scripture doesn't say, "Your education will make room for you." Now, I fully believe in educating yourself, but if education alone was the secret to a fulfilled life, then everyone with a degree would be living out the best version of themselves. Today's statistics on career fulfillment prove otherwise. Gallup surveys show that over 60% of the working population across all career tracks, educational levels, and industries are "not engaged" or are "actively disengaged" from their work. It's not that we, as a whole, have lost our ability to connect with meaningful work. I believe the answer to this disengagement is the fact that most of us are not living out our purpose. The work we are doing might be meaningful to the right person, but not to us!

When we actively suppress the part of our being that wants to dream and grow, and instead, force ourselves onto paths that we imagine to be less risky or more practical, we are settling for a life we were never meant to live. You can have all the education in the world, but if you're not actively reaching toward your individual life purpose, something will always feel 'off.' It is that unsatisfied gnawing that many of us can't put our finger on.

The good news here is that your 'why' is right where you left it and you can pick it up at any moment. You have an internal compass that can still be accessed. It's the place where your dreams are still alive.

So, the question then is, "Where is my why and how do I find it?"

Your journey to your 'why' truly begins when you make that first decision in awareness. The moment you say to yourself, "I will give myself permission to find and live out my life purpose," the entire universe conspires together to bring it to pass. You move from darkness to light by one choice. The follow-up actions and steps you will take will reveal themselves along the way.

It begins with the decision to actively disengage from everyone else's expectations and allow yourself to fully access that inner child who was allowed to dream big.

Think about it. Do you remember the last time you woke up with a true sense of purpose, or have you been operating as a slave to the deadlines and the constant flood of distractions offered up by the influences around you? Remember, in an earlier chapter you learned that you have to be the bouncer of your own brain. It goes deeper than just focusing on positive thoughts and believing in yourself. You also have to agree to protect the vision and purpose that you've been given, even if it hasn't fully revealed itself yet.

It's as simple as this: The key to walking is to continue to walk. Once you decide to live out your purpose, you will naturally find yourself in positions where you will have opportunities to choose to nurture your dreams. You will also have opportunities to suppress them. It is a continual choice you are making with every step.

"But how will I know?"

This is where most people get stuck. Many of us aren't used to accessing our internal compass. It seems too New Age to nurture an unknown path. "What if I make a mistake? What if I fail?" See the vicious cycle? That kind of thinking will have you right back in the grip of fear. Fear of the unknown is what keeps us in the bondage of settling for far less than we were created to be.

The truth is, you don't have to know exactly how it will all come together, and I can promise you that you won't! Your biggest responsibility in this process of becoming is to choose to say yes to your purpose every day without putting a cap on your dreams.

Everything else will come to you. Why? Because as you begin to say yes to your true purpose and give yourself permission to live free from the prison you've put yourself in, you will begin to see your goals and dreams with ever increasing clarity. The fact that you want to see them is all it takes for them to begin to appear. The more you say yes, the more will be revealed. You've only been stuck all this time because you made a decision to leave your dreams and goals behind. You lost your 'why' when you traded your purpose for something that seemed easier or more secure.

Compromise will always be offered to you, so get used to that. But as you continue to live a life intent on fulfilling your purpose, the voices of the things you used to settle for will begin to sound more ridiculous.

It's like the guy who pushed against all odds to become the first entrepreneur in his family. He started out cutting his neighbor's lawn, and now ten years later he has seven crews who are responsible for all the golf-course properties in his town. What would happen if someone walked up to him and offered him a secure management job with an hourly pay rate? If entrepreneurship is connected to his 'why' and he is living out his purpose, he would laugh at that offer. Sure, it may seem like less work, less responsibility, and a guaranteed paycheck, but in reality, this man's passion is already attached to his business. He is fulfilled. He is continuing to grow. In fact, he just provided two jobs last month to young men who are in the community re-entry program. These men served time in prison and now are receiving a second chance at life. This extra layer of fulfillment further connects this entrepreneur to his 'why.' Do you think he knew he'd be helping change lives when he first felt that inner pull to start his own lawn service company? Of course not, but he had the courage to follow his inner compass. He decided to say yes to that pull.

Where is your inner compass pointing you? If you choose to listen and continue to give yourself permission to live out your greatest purpose, you will find it, because it's already within you.

If one advances confidently in the direction of one's dreams, and endeavors to live the life which one has imagined, one will meet with a success unexpected in common hours.

~ Henry David Thoreau

ACTION EXERCISES

Do you know why you are here?

Are you happy in knowing why you are here?

Do you know anyone who passionately pursues his or her purpose?

What difference does it make in their life?

If you don't know your purpose, are you spending some time every day looking for it?

Write out the answers, or think about them, or better yet, discuss them with a loved one.

13

SUMMARY

God doesn't require us to succeed; He only requires that you try.

~ Mother Teresa

If you've got this far through the book, I'm guessing you're ready for the next marvelous chapter of your life. It's time for a change, right? Another ten years on autopilot is just not an option anymore.

In this chapter, I've tried to use the words, mainly paraphrased, of some of the greatest contributors to personal growth.

I used to lie in bed thinking to myself, 'I wonder what I'm capable of doing if I really throw myself into something with all my might?'

And it was a comforting thought for a while. It took me away from the humdrum of my daily, disappointing existence; but inevitably I had to return at some point.

The interesting thing was that I somehow thought that the only requirement for my dream life to unfold was for me to be discovered, that someone would spot my genius and then everything would be alright! How can you delude yourself to that extent?

Eventually, I came to the realization that nothing is going to happen unless I make it happen. No one is going to discover you, no one is going to make it easy for you, no one is going to take away the pain. You have to do it for yourself.

For some people that might be bad news. But when you think about it, it means that your new life can begin any moment you choose. You are not waiting for anyone.

Your life may be dark and disappointing, but hope begins in the dark.

You may be worried about failing. You may be concerned about being disappointed if things don't work out, as you wanted. Well, you will be disappointed because you will fail. But failure is temporary if you keep going. And what's the alternative? You are certainly doomed if you don't even try.

You may be worried about what other people will say. And it's true, you may well be in for ridicule and criticism from those who lack your courage not to settle for a stagnant life. But those who never make a mistake — never try anything new — never take the plunge, well, they never reach a fulfilling life. The only way to avoid criticism is to do nothing, say nothing, and be nothing. And it's obvious where that will lead.

You may berate yourself for not having started this years ago; surely it's too late now. But no matter how old you are, you have the rest of your life ahead of you. It is pure folly not to go after a goal because of the amount of time it will take to achieve it. The time is going to pass anyway!

Maybe you could have started years ago. Perhaps the very best time to begin would have been ten or even twenty years ago. But you didn't, so the second-best time is right now. It's never too late to become what you could have been!

"Too many of us are not living our dreams because we are too busy living our fears."

~ Les Brown

Why don't more of us go for it then? Les Brown is right when he says that too many of us are not living our dreams because we are living our fears. (He also said, "The tiger doesn't concern himself with the opinion of the sheep!" Although it doesn't fit here, I love it!)

We just can't afford to allow fear to hold us back. We have to find a way to go after our dreams, because if we don't, then we will spend our time working for someone else, building their dreams for them.

We don't need to be a genius and we don't need to be an overnight success. It doesn't matter how long it takes us or how slowly we go, as long as we don't give up. As long as we don't stop.

We need to find the motivation to keep moving forward, to go from one failure to the next with no loss of enthusiasm.

The more we persist, the more we develop character, and character is ours to keep. Your business or job will never out-perform you. The only way for the work to get better is for you to get better at constantly working on yourself and your character.

You need to take the plunge!

If we are going to be successful in living out our dream life, then we have to stand up straight and look life in the eye. We need to take part. We need to take the plunge!

How do we become so paralyzed and unadventurous in adult life? Why are we so worried about messing up, making mistakes or appearing foolish?

As my mentor, John Maxwell says, "No one is good at anything the first time." So, if we are going to try new things, we are going to mess up, and that's ok! That's good!

As we take part in life, we learn and grow. But I'm talking about more than just doing something different. Continual growth is transformational. It is the difference between doing something different and becoming someone different. I believe that's why we're here — to experience life and to learn and grow from our experiences. We are three-dimensional beings (mind, body, and spirit). Continuous growth in each dimension is essential for a fulfilled life. If we neglect one of the three parts of our being, it can and will affect the other two.

My personal mission statement is….

To think, act, and live a life of quality character, pursuing greatness that's pleasing and acceptable to my Creator, so that I can be a positive influence on each person I meet, and the difference maker in the lives of those who know me best.

I believe that our responsibility is to think, act, and pursue our dreams. And, we don't need to worry about doing it perfectly. We are responsible for the effort, not the result. We can't control a great deal about the world and all the other people in it, but we can control our own efforts. We can all do our best, and that's all it takes.

Please remember that you were designed for a purpose and to live a life of significance. Life's too short for you to waste time with a negative attitude. I remember not long ago that my mom made a comment about my attitude. She said, "You never get 'down' do you? You're always 'up' and motivated, aren't you?" She went on to say that she remembered that no matter the upsets in my life, I never let them keep me on the ground. I told her, "If you think about it, it's really a waste of time to be any other way!" It is also extremely counterproductive. It is my hope that each of you who has read this book would ponder that statement that I made to mom. Isn't it really a waste of time and a waste of this short life to be a negative person? If you are typically a negative person, how has that worked out for you so far?

I believe that the best explanation (in my opinion) of true success came from Zig Ziglar. I memorized it for the purpose of closing out my training sessions. He told a story of visiting his mother in the nursing home, and how his wife (as he referred to as 'Sugar Baby') would just hug the patients and say, "I love you!" and then tell them that if they needed anything to not hesitate to ask. Zig, of course, had the intention of walking in and sharing inspiring words of encouragement and wisdom. When he observed 'Sugar Baby's' actions, he went outside and broke down into tears. He knew at that moment that they needed her, and his actions would pale compared the actions of his wife. He then sat down and pinned the words of what true success means. If the following does not inspire you, then you need a brain or a heart transplant:

When Do You Know You're a Success?

You're a success when you make friends with your past, are focused on the present, and optimistic about the future. You're a success when you've made friends with your adversaries, and have gained the love and respect of those who know you best; when you're filled with faith, hope, and love, and live without anger, greed, guilt, envy, or thoughts of revenge; when you know that failure to stand for what is morally right is the prelude to being the victim of what is criminally wrong. You're a success when you're mature enough to delay gratification and shift your focus away from your rights and onto your responsibilities. You're a success when you love the unlovable, give hope to the hopeless, friendship to the friendless, and encouragement to the discouraged; when you know that success (a win) doesn't make you, and failure (a loss) doesn't break you. You're a success when you can look back in forgiveness, forward in hope, down in compassion, and up with gratitude; when you clearly understand that failure is an event, not a person — that yesterday ended last night, and today is your brand-new day; when you know that he who would be the greatest among you must become the servant of all. You're a success when you're pleasant to the grouch, courteous to the rude, and generous to the needy, because you know that the long-term benefit of giving and forgiving far outweigh the short-term benefits of receiving and revenge. You're a success when you recognize, confess, develop, and use your God given physical, mental, and spiritual abilities for the glory of God and to the benefit of mankind. When you can one day stand in front of the Creator of the universe, and He says to you, "Well done, my good and faithful servant."

I apologize to Zig's family if the quote was not exactly right. I transcribed it from one of his audio recordings years ago. My memory may have missed some of the words.

As I was writing this chapter and Zig Ziglar's success description, waves of guilt permeated my heart, and I knew that I had to forgive and ask forgiveness of others from recent events in my life. Life sometimes has a paradoxical way of teaching us valuable lessons. None of us can totally be free if we harbor bitterness and unforgiveness in our hearts. I thank God for His timely intervention, and one day I'll thank Zig Ziglar for being part of my life on this earth.

You know for each of us eventually, life will come to an end. There will be no more sunrises, no minutes, hours or days. All the things you collected, whether treasured or forgotten, will pass to someone else. Your wealth, fame, and temporal power will shrivel to irrelevance. It won't matter what you owned or owed. Your grudges, resentments, and frustrations will finally disappear. So too, your hopes, ambitions, plans, and to do lists will expire. The wins and losses that once seemed so important will just go away. It won't matter where you came from or what political party you belonged to at the end. It won't matter if you're beautiful or a genius, or even what nation you call home. So, what will matter? How will the value of your days be measured?

What will matter is not what you bought but what you built — not what you got but what you gave. What will matter is not your success but your significance. What will matter is not what you learned but what you taught. What will matter is every act of integrity, compassion, courage, or sacrifice that enriched, empowered, or encouraged others to emulate your example. What will matter is not so much your competence but your character. What will matter is not how many people you knew, but how many will feel a lasting loss when you're gone. What will matter is not your memories, but the memories that live on in those who knew you and love you. What will matter is how long you will be remembered by whom and for what. A life lived that matters is not of circumstance but of choice.

Did that writing I shared above move you emotionally? I know that when I heard something like it from a speaker, it inspired me to expound on it and write about what matters most at the end of our days. I hope it inspires you as well. The greatest affect you will have on others is often felt the most when your gone.

Time is not on your side. Get motivated and get inspired! You are running the show. Your God-given independent will was instilled in you for a purpose. As Zig Ziglar so eloquently put it, "God don't make no junk!"

May God bless you on your journey, and may you recognize His grace and mercy. Start now and go as far as you can see, and when you get there, you'll see how to go further.

Thank you for buying this book and reading it! Now it's time to "Take the Plunge!"

This book will soon be on audio along with other audio programs to inspire you to true education. Learning how to unlearn is true education. The true meaning of 'education' is not acquiring knowledge. The Latin-English Dictionary is the true definition: "To draw out, lead out, march out/bring up."

I can't wait to start on my new book. I have already created a journal specifically for it.

If you would like to find out more about some of my other learning resources and training programs, I'd love to work with you or your organization. If I do work for your organization, I give a money back guarantee on anything I deliver. You can contact me at….

www.JohnMaxwellGroup.com/randyperdue

randyperdue1@yahoo.com

or

perduerandy58@gmail.com

"If I had a dollar for every time I got distracted, man, I'd love some ice cream right now! Is that a chicken over there?" Oops! Forgot to take my medication!"

Made in the USA
Lexington, KY
19 May 2017